To Jo fro[...]

with mu[...]

thoughts

neiges d'antan and

all that.

April 1969.

'THAT INFIDEL PLACE'

A SHORT HISTORY OF
GIRTON COLLEGE
1869–1969

The Foundress, Emily Davies

'THAT INFIDEL PLACE'

A SHORT HISTORY OF GIRTON COLLEGE 1869–1969

WITH AN ESSAY ON THE COLLEGIATE UNIVERSITY IN THE MODERN WORLD

By

M. C. BRADBROOK, Litt.D.

Mistress of Girton College and Professor of English Literature, Cambridge University

WITH AN INTRODUCTION BY

LORD BUTLER OF SAFFRON WALDEN

Master of Trinity College, Cambridge

1969

CHATTO AND WINDUS

LONDON

Published by
Chatto & Windus Ltd
42 William IV Street
London W.C.2
★
Clarke, Irwin & Co. Ltd
Toronto

SBN: 7011 1344 8

Printed in Great Britain
by Cox and Wyman Ltd
London, Fakenham and Reading

CONTENTS

ILLUSTRATIONS

FOREWORD

Where a collegiate university does not yet exist, it is regarded as an ideal.

Where it has existed longest, colleges are liable to attack, as closed circles of privilege – even while new colleges appear within the same university.

Fantastic notions of wealth and irresponsibility may be entertained even by professional sociologists of other institutions, when they speak of the colleges of Oxford or Cambridge.* Yet simultaneously, in rich societies like California, or in less rich ones like South Australia, many English-speaking nations are looking to Oxford and Cambridge for a new model to redress the difficulties they encounter.

To set the history of one women's college in this wider context may not seem inappropriate or presumptuous, since colleges, like other educational communities, sometimes can be self-sufficient but are inevitably also interrelated. Moreover, the foundation of the College for Women, a hundred years ago, coincided with a wide educational movement; its centenary falls near that of many universities in distant parts of the English-speaking world.

In such pioneer communities, colleges represented the contribution of private interests and appeared as a modification within state institutions, sometimes of greater but elsewhere of merely subordinate interest. In Oxford and Cambridge, where colleges were originally cells in a larger, a more international community, each was at this time a corporation enjoying self-government and special privileges.

When Girton was founded, the Cambridge colleges were

* See the article by Peter Collison in *The Illustrated London News* for 23rd July, 1966, dealing with Clare College.

exceptionally powerful and the university exceptionally weak; had the university been stronger, such an unofficial penetration of its examination system, and such an undefined form of association as persisted for many years would hardly have been possible; nor would a corporation, however small and ill-endowed, but founded on the collegiate model, have been able to achieve such innovations.

Girton College, the earliest institution for women at Oxford or Cambridge, was founded on the clear principle of aiming at the highest education, without any modification or concessions to the inexperience of women; and for this principle large sacrifices were made. Once founded, it aimed at the rapid expansion of numbers to meet the social needs for educated women. The present number of undergraduates (1968–9) is 350, graduates about 60, and the fellowship some 55, including four Fellows of the Royal Society.

To meet the national need for more women at Cambridge, a considerable expansion is planned (see below, p. 85) on a new central site, which will provide Cambridge with the equivalent of a fourth college for women.

The aim of the founders is still the aim today; in the following pages, the story of our college is told in some detail, both for its own value to Girtonians in particular and women in general. Some of its connexions, affiliations and analogues are suggested in the final chapter. The views expressed here are purely personal, and should not be read as an expression of policy for Girton College.

The Principal of Newnham kindly read the proofs, saving me from some errors.

Cambridge, 1968   M. C. Bradbrook

INTRODUCTION

As the new Mistress of Girton, Professor Bradbrook has done a great service in writing a book on the College in celebration of the centenary in 1969. She regards the first two parts of the book on the College for Women and the Social Image as 'just family – or at least just feminist – history'. This is to underestimate the charm of these early chapters. It is in fact on the early Part that many readers will concentrate in reading of Girton and in particular about the Girton Girl in Chapter Five. A princely intruder in feminine disguise discusses the future syllabus with the Mistress, and from then on we are regaled by a series of lyrical descriptions which should not be missed.

It is, however, in her last part on the collegiate university that Professor Bradbrook is most original. She says in her foreword that in rich societies like California, or in less rich ones like South Australia, many English-speaking nations are looking to Oxford and Cambridge for a model to redress the difficulties they encounter. This is why the author sets Girton in a wide context involving California, Australia and a great many other places as well. She makes the point that the foundation a hundred years ago coincided with a wide education movement. The centenary coincides with many problems of what she describes as the new collegiate university. Where I think the reader will have to exercise discernment is in the use of the word 'College'. Professor Bradbrook is clearly much seized with the importance of California and although Clark Kerr talks about a cell developing in California which expands into a larger whole yet keeping its identity, the fact is that the mere size of such an institution is so immense that comparisons with Cambridge and its real collegiate system are very difficult.

The number of graduates at Girton, however, is sixty compared with the total of three hundred and fifty. It is to be anticipated that under her rule, the number of graduates will increase. She feels that Girton, which was originally founded to establish the right of women to the same intellectual training as men, may discover a further duty to protect the special interests of women where they begin to consider the differentiating aspects of their intellectual life rather than those which they share with men. She has some amusing things to say about the shaping of college life and mentions the recent article in the Cambridge Review, by Jack Goody, 'Is Your Master really necessary?'

She quotes Bodin on education and goes on to see conflict between the 'Community Natural' and 'Community Civil' which may be further traced in that apparent inconsistency, which drives some junior members to demand adult status within the community and simultaneously the kind of personal and individual attention from their teachers which is due to a favourite son. This aptly sums up the problem of our youth today and Professor Bradbrook says that as Mistress of Girton she will watch over the susceptibilities of youth. I detect a certain anxiety in her attitude which may derive from her experience in California. I think she will find Girton not too large a 'cell' and certainly a rewarding one. Perhaps she will have the compliment paid to her as has been paid to Clark Kerr 'He's a father, if a bad father' for which we may substitute in her case the word mother, 'and a good mother'.   BUTLER

Part I

THE COLLEGE FOR WOMEN

Chapter 1

MISS ELIZABETH GARRETT, MISS EMILY DAVIES, AND WOMEN'S EDUCATION IN THE 1860s

I

'HA! this is Hitchin, and that, I believe, is the house where the College for Women is: that *infidel* place!' Accents of clerical disapproval fell authoritatively upon the speaker's two female companions as the heavily upholstered railway carriage drew out of Hitchin station. A little Quakeress who had just seated herself blushed deeply: 'Oh, no! not infidel! why do you say that?' she pleaded: was it not founded on the same principles as the men's colleges at Cambridge?

Anna Lloyd could hardly have been surprised when she saw the recoil with which the ladies eyed her; for when at the age of thirty she had decided to join the College for Women, her own sisters had expressed much the same astonishment and horror; 'How worldly! how shocking!' they had exclaimed; even 'how unchristian!'[*]

Nevertheless Miss Lloyd had arrived at Benslow House when the doors opened on 16 October 1869, where with four other young women she was received by a small, neat, middle-aged lady 'quivering with excitement, thinly veiled under a business-like manner'. Miss Emily Davies wrote to her London friends that 'our little band of undergraduates

[*] *Anna Lloyd, A Memoir* by Edyth Lloyd, 1928. p. 57. Emily Davies at first thought her 'amusing and original' and later 'most valuable'.

3

seem to be coming in the best possible *tone*! If not numerous, they are certainly select,' for she had felt from the moment of seeing them at the Entrance Examination in July that 'they looked like discreet young women' and that 'there is not one as to whom there need be any fear that she would do anything foolish'.* Of course they were not to be exposed to the dangers of living in Cambridge; Hitchin in Hertfordshire was twenty-six miles away, and the Cambridge gentlemen, all rather regrettably young, who had volunteered to lecture, must be prepared to spend three hours on journeying for the sake of the cause. Even so, kind Mr Seebohm the banker, their next neighbour and a good friend, did not permit his daughters to join; though the youngest, Miss Emily Seebohm, in her old age recalled to me the pleasure of playing in the shrubberies with the pretty young ladies.

The project was felt by many to be impious, morally shocking, because it would distract women from home duties. For this reason, the daughters of the Headmaster of Marlborough could not be entered, in spite of Miss Davies's eloquent plea to their mother. Miss Lloyd, though an orphan and without home duties of any kind, was persuaded to withdraw after four terms. Her family, while not prepared to make a fixed home for her, still regarded membership of the College for Women as a life 'merely of self-indulgence and self-satisfaction, distracting her from the plain duties that lay before her'† – duties which now seem far from evident. It was true that Miss Lloyd had no need to earn her bread, and that she had no programme of examinations in view. But after one term she told Miss Davies that she understood more clearly the scholarly way of looking at things as compared with that of the man of business; and she later

* Barbara Stephen, *Emily Davies and Girton College*, 1927, p. 218, p. 216.
† *Anna Lloyd*, p. 71.

Barbara Bodichon

Henry Tomkinson

Henrietta Maria,
Lady Stanley of Alderley

knew that what she had absorbed at Girton became a source
of joy for the rest of her life. More especially, she had learnt
to appreciate art from one of her fellow students, a great
admirer of William Morris and the Pre-Raphaelites; and so
she became a friend and pupil of John Ruskin.

For these young women, the delights of privacy, the
chance of knowledge for its own sake opened a glorious
prospect. The most brilliant of them said 'she had for the
last three months felt her life worth something; she had not
cared so much about it before.'* Another, hearing of the
college, thought '*That's* what you have been waiting for!',
and would wake every morning 'with a sort of sting of
delight and think "A whole other day in this lovely
College!"'†

Delight and enhancement of existence sprang directly
from the removal of a dead weight of disability – the assumption that a woman was inherently debarred from the
intellectual life. 'I have nothing but pity and contempt for
all female scribblers,' wrote Monk Lewis, a minor novelist
contemporary with Jane Austen; 'The needle and not the
pen is the implement they should use and the only one they
employ with dexterity.'

To remove prejudice masked as Christian ethics, assumptions disguised as intellectual convictions, an equal mixture
of courage, passionate commitment and administrative skill
was required.

The tough Evangelical piety of Emily Davies, daughter
of the late Rector of Gateshead, had been tested by twenty
years' parish work; in drawing up a possible list of committee

* Ibid, p. 59. This was the future Dame Louisa Innes Lumsden, first
Head Mistress of St Leonards School, St Andrews.
† This was Constance Maynard, first Mistress of Westfield College,
London. See C. B. Firth, *Constance Louisa Maynard*, 1949, p. 114.

members for her college, she had marked off each of them for some desirable quality, ending 'E. D. – Principles'. In this, Miss Davies underestimated herself. She had seen a vision of society, a whole way of life, for women, a kind of New Jerusalem:

> O *sweet and blessed College,*
> *The home of the elect*

as she ironically wrote to a friend.

The distinguishing quality of Emily Davies, as of Florence Nightingale, was to combine her vision of the New Jerusalem with gifts for organisation, administration and practical detail; she would have shone as Secretary of State, or the Governor of a Colony. In spite of her tireless energy, her work was impersonal. Herself no scholar, she was prepared to sacrifice the natural development of the individual students to conform to an ideal. She could be utterly intransigent and disastrously mistaken. Yet the driving force which she alone commanded was that which brought the New Jerusalem down to Hitchin Hill.

The students were to call her 'the little instigator'.

In all matters other than women's education, Emily Davies was perfectly conventional – indeed a stickler for proprieties. Her young ladies were to behave like young ladies, while at the same time they were to omit nothing, absolutely nothing, from their course of study, which was required of undergraduates. Her insistence on the first brought her occasionally into conflict with the students; her insistence on the second involved her more frequently in disputes with her co-founders and supporters.

'No,' one aged lady observed meditatively to me about twenty years ago, 'we were never militant – not what I would call militant.'

6

In the 1860s there would have been little hope for a movement of rebels led by radicals like Mary Wollstonecraft, or eccentrics like the Ladies of Llangollen. A strong mixture of diplomacy was required – diplomacy, the art of the possible. This was supplied by Emily Davies (when her principles were not engaged) and powerfully by Henry Richard Tomkinson, who was included in the committee for that important quality 'conciliation'. A product of Rugby and Trinity, a Wrangler and a Blue, ex-Bursar of Marlborough, managing director of the Sun Life Insurance Office, Tomkinson possessed greater influence over Miss Davies than anyone else, and was more deeply trusted. As Miss Davies produced her project, he scribbled a frivolous note on his agenda:

Polly, B.A.

His conciliation – even more, his sense of humour – was needed both to combat outside prejudice and to reconcile the conflicting ideals of Miss Davies and her little band.

Perhaps this quality extended to the students; that Miss Lloyd was not without the art of sweet persuasion may be deduced from her report that 'the clergyman, as he left the train, shook hands and said he was glad I could give such a good account of affairs'.

The founding of the College for Women was part of a national movement which took many forms; different aspects of the women's cause, centred in London and the great cities of the industrial north, became linked with other national movements for the reform of education in schools and universities, and for improving the standard of the teaching profession. Educational and economic opportunities were the first need; social and political freedom followed when these were conceded.

As different groups followed different interests, they might find that co-operation was not possible – that indeed they became rivals. One of the commonest causes of a split – being closely entangled with education – was religion, where advanced views ranged from agnosticism to disestablishment. The forces brought to play at the time of the foundation of the College for Women proved extremely complex.

This first foundation holds a special significance because the object was particularly bold, simple and uncompromising. An experiment was carried out in its purest form. There was no doubt about the aim, and after 1873 there was no doubt about the achievement either. Other experiments may have been better designed, more immediately sympathetic, more adaptable; Miss Davies's achievement had the distinction of being unrepeatable. Like the first ascent of an unconquered peak, the first crossing of an uncharted territory, the College for Women set up the standard against which all later effort must inevitably be measured. 'You see, it won't do to blow the trumpet with an uncertain sound,' she wrote to her Newcastle confidante (a sort of honorary sister named Anna Richardson).

Miss Davies was the daughter and the sister of clerical schoolmasters.* 'Our education answered to that of clergymen's daughters generally,' she wrote. 'They have lessons and get on as they can.' She wrote weekly themes for her father, and learnt Latin with her brothers; Anna Richardson tried to teach her a little Greek. Her father, the son of a Welsh farmer, for his love of Latin nicknamed 'Horace

---

* Lord Llewelyn-Davies is the present representative of the family, the great great nephew of Emily Davies.

bach' by the Cardiganshire neighbours, had been at Queens'
College, Cambridge, Miss Davies's favourite brother,
Llewelyn, was at Repton and Trinity; when he took orders,
he moved to London and became deeply influenced by the
Christian Socialism of Frederick Denison Maurice. This was
a more radical form of Christianity than Miss Davies had
yet known, but she was drawn into the group and, after her
father's death in 1862, finally settled near Llewelyn, now
Rector of Marylebone. She was never required to earn her
living, but her income was very small; if she went to call on
great ladies and felt she must buy a new bonnet, then she had
to stop buying books.

She knew already several people engaged in work for
women, on questions of employment, the franchise and
education. At first she took part in these efforts; it seems possible that she was led to concentrate on education by her
great friendship with the first woman to qualify as a medical
practitioner in England. To this single and lonely figure,
Emily Davies gave a warm personal sympathy which she
never extended to any of her own students. Elizabeth Garrett, whom she had met in 1859 when they were both brides-
maids to Annie Crow (a future Mistress of Girton College),
had chosen a profession where standards were defined, protected, unambiguous; and she shared Emily Davies's refusal
to compromise.

She learnt the determined, quiet politeness that did not
flinch before rage or snub; and she also dressed beautifully
and looked elegant. 'I feel so mean trying to win over the
doctors by all kinds of feminine dodges,' she confessed to
Emily.

Though five years had passed since Miss Nightingale had
sailed for Scutari and proceeded to order the affairs of the
British Army's medical service, the image of a gentle Lady

with a Lamp conveniently disguised from the public the 'masculine resolution' which Emily Davies recognised in her work.★ A favourite anagram 'Flit on, cheering angel' represented the idea of what she had done. Helped by Llewelyn and Emily Davies, Miss Garrett set off for the Middlesex Hospital under the fiction of taking a nurse's training. When she was there she wrote very fully to Emily Davies, and accepted her advice on how to plan the campaign. The long, devious route by which she found unguarded ways to the heart of 'the Fortress' – ways which were usually closed as soon as she had revealed their existence† – must have shown more clearly than anything else that the need of women was for a college of their own; but a college which allowed exactly the same opportunities as those given to men. The six years' struggle of Elizabeth Garrett taught Emily Davies what her own life work was to be. Before it was half over, Miss Davies was herself in London, learning how to get things done.

There is a story that one night in 1860, Emily Davies, on a visit to Elizabeth Garrett's home, sat by the firelight in Elizabeth's bedroom while they brushed their hair together. 'Well, Elizabeth,' she said, 'it is clear what has to be done. I must devote myself to securing higher education while you open the medical profession for women. After these things are done, we must see about getting the vote.' She turned to Elizabeth's small sister, sitting quietly beside them on a stool: 'You are younger than we are, Millie,' she observed to the

★ Miss Nightingale's copy of John Stuart Mill's *The Subjection of Women* (1869), heavily marked, is in Girton College Library. Her terrifying *Cassandra* (1859) was printed in Ray Strachey's *The Cause* (1928).
† See Jo Manton, *Elizabeth Garrett Anderson, a Biography*, 1965.

future Dame Millicent Fawcett, 'so you must attend to that.'*

The fifties had been an intensely active decade in the advance of women's employment, and in the question of married women's legal rights, especially their rights to property, as well as in educational questions. In 1851, on marrying Harriet Taylor, John Stuart Mill had signed a document renouncing the rights which the law conferred on him over her 'person, property and freedom of action'. But early agitation on this subject did not succeed. Educational advance was more promising. As early as 1848, Frederick Denison Maurice had started a College in London under the auspices of the Governesses' Benevolent Institution, where ladies attended lectures on a variety of subjects; a school for girls was also attached to it. The next year a wealthy Unitarian widow opened a similar establishment on non-denominational lines. Ladies trained at Queen's College, Harley Street, and the College in Bedford Square soon began founding schools; Frances Mary Buss started the North London Collegiate School in 1850; five years later, the Ladies' College, Cheltenham, early to come under the rule of Dorothea Beale, was set up in that town; while in the north Miss Anne Jemima Clough started small schools at Liverpool and Ambleside.

The next requisite was university qualifications for teachers. In the absence of any official channel of expression, the various movements were connected chiefly through the interests of one or two devoted persons. Women had become used to writing but they had not the instruments for any corporate action. Educational ferment threw up all kinds of

* Ibid, p. 72. The story is probably fictitious; Miss Davies called her friend Lizzie.

experiments in London – *The Englishwoman's Journal*, the Social Science Association, the Society for Promoting the Employment of Women (founded 1859), an Employment Agency for women; people met in little circles in drawing-rooms of Kensington and Cambridge and Liverpool. It must have been very difficult to distinguish the promising from the eccentric, the viable from the fore-doomed. Series of lectures were started for the educationally underprivileged, whether these were the working classes, or the women, or budding scientists. 'The origin of the movement was intellectual, not economic, bourgeois not proletarian', wrote Halévy, 'and its political outlook was conservative.'

The lady who gave her name to the epoch was willing to extend her patronage to a school that aimed at raising the standard of governesses' education, and Queen's College, Harley Street, gained a Royal Charter by 1853. The education of girls was accepted; any political moves roused the absolute temper of the constitutional monarch.

> The Queen is most anxious to enlist everyone who can speak or write to join in checking this mad, wicked folly of 'Women's rights' with all its attendant horrors, on which her poor feeble sex is bent, forgetting every sense of womanly feeling and propriety . . . It is a subject which makes the Queen so furious she can not contain herself . . . The Queen is sure that Mrs Martin agrees with her.*

Emily Davies, who in a number of ways bore a likeness to Queen Victoria – small, obstinate and highly conventional – added to her campaigning gifts a clear, trenchant and forcible style. Between 1860 and 1868 she published papers on women's employment and education, and read others to the

* Sir Theodore Martin, *Queen Victoria as I knew Her*, pp. 69–70. Lady Amberley, daughter of Lady Stanley (a founder of Girton) caused this outburst. 'Lady A. deserves a good whipping' wrote the Queen.

Social Science Association of which she was secretary. When, in 1866, John Stuart Mill organised a petition to Parliament asking for the franchise to be opened to women, it was signed by Florence Nightingale, Harriet Martineau, Mary Somerville, Josephine Butler, with 1,499 names in all, and carried to Westminster Hall by Miss Emily Davies and Miss Elizabeth Garrett (while waiting for Mill, they hid it on an applewoman's stall). After this, fearing the effect upon her campaign for women's education, Emily Davies withdrew from direct efforts for the vote, and the wisdom of the move was to be shown later. In the same way, Miss Garrett also had to proceed with extreme caution, while few people who had causes of their own to further could support Josephine Butler in her courageous work for prostitutes: Miss Garrett, indeed, opposed it. Educational reform held first place till the end of the 1880s.

II

Miss Davies began working for education in a general way; to raise the level of teaching for girls, it was necessary to raise the level of teachers. In her very first publication, Miss Davies sarcastically pointed out that to keep a school was the refuge of any female, however uneducated, who was left without means of support; for nothing else, except the greater misery of the seamstress, was open to her. She thought young women might be trained as clerks, that they might be used more widely in shopkeeping and in certain kinds of manufacture.* Later, she conducted a survey into the employment of women in the Newcastle area, where domestic

* Emily Davies, *Questions Relating to Women*, ed. E. E. C. Jones, 1910, pp. 11–12.

service represented promotion over some of the rough labouring work that women performed.

When Queen's College was founded in 1848, it had been an attempt to improve governesses' training: the dismal life of these unfortunates had provided the subject for many novels by that date. Jane Austen's *Emma* (1816) is the study of a young woman's self-education; for if Emma had enjoyed the friendship of an excellent governess, Miss Taylor, trained in 'the school of adversity', what Miss Taylor taught her was chiefly 'principles'. Jane Fairfax, trained by 'the best masters in London', attained a far higher standard of accomplishment but was herself destined for 'the governess trade' and proposed at twenty-one to 'retire from all the pleasures of rational intercourse, equal society, peace and hope, to penance and mortification for ever'. (By this fate, which required 'something more than human perfection of body and mind to be discharged with tolerable comfort', Jane Austen herself may have felt threatened.) Much lower in the educational scale, however, comes Mrs Goddard's school, 'a real old-fashioned boarding-school . . . where girls might be sent to be out of the way, and scramble themselves into a little education without any danger of coming back prodigies'; so that in her boredom Emma undertakes in an amateur way the further education of Mrs Goddard's parlour-boarder, Harriet Smith.

Thirty years or so later, Charlotte Brontë was writing of the wrongs and woes of a governess from direct knowledge. Her governesses are highly trained, by comparison with Jane Austen's, but their social position is even worse; and in *Vanity Fair* – published the same year as *Jane Eyre* – Thackeray exposed 'the governess trade' in a cooler fashion but perhaps more effectually.

When the plans for Queen's College, Harley Street, were

put forward in 1846 by the Governesses' Benevolent Institution, *Punch* commented ironically:

> To the Institute will be attached a Servants' Hall, wherein at stated times, will attend a number of footmen and other menials, to intercourse with whom the future governess may be habituated, and whose insults and impertinences she may learn betimes to put up with . . . The children will drop in every now and then, daily, and reprimand and find fault capriciously and unjustly with their preceptress, so as to inure her to any such treatment.*

A year after Miss Davies published her survey, the extraordinarily popular *East Lynne* appeared, where the supreme humiliation of Mrs Henry Wood's fallen heroine, Lady Isobel, is to return (heavily disguised) as governess to her own children after her husband has married Another.

In 1863, things began moving fast. Miss Davies succeeded in getting the Cambridge Local Examinations temporarily thrown open to girls' schools. (It was as secretary of the London Centre that Henry Tomkinson met Miss Davies and became her life-long friend.) Though Miss Beale did not approve, Miss Buss and some other headmistresses sent in enough candidates to justify the experiment, which showed that in subjects other than mathematics girls in good schools were tolerably well taught. There was now an external standard to be aimed at, if only it might be retained permanently.

Next, some Cambridge men were invited to public meetings – 'especially enemies, to give them a chance of being converted'. Three lovely girls were put in the front row, no one who looked 'strong-minded' was to be given any

* See *Queen's College, 1848–1948*, by R. G. Grylls, 1948, pp. 12–13.

prominence, but Elizabeth Garrett would be very useful, for she looked 'exactly like one of those girls whose instinct is to do what you tell them'.* The permanent right was conceded. Two years later, in February 1866, Miss Davies organised the London School-mistresses' Association, of which she became secretary. The schools thus gained a way of exerting pressure and exchanging views.

Meanwhile, between 1864 and 1866 there had been a Government Commission of Inquiry on Schools. This was Miss Davies's great chance. She pointed out that girls' schools were not being considered. It was one of her strong points that many charity foundations spent nearly all their income on the boys' schools, and did hardly anything for girls. (Christ's Hospital was especially lax.) After a fierce but short dispute girls were included; Miss Davies, Miss Beale and Miss Buss were called to testify. Women had never done anything like this before; the Committee were much impressed by their womanliness and by the tears in the eyes of Miss Beale. Miss Beale in her time had taught in the notorious Clergy Daughters' School, which is supposed to be the original of Lowood School in *Jane Eyre*. The Report gave a mass of needed information – this was an age of blue books and statistics – and the ladies gained more valuable allies, such as James Bryce and H. J. Roby.

Finally (the documents are now at Girton, written in Miss Davies's neat firm hand), she took up the role that was to be hers for thirty-seven years.

A Meeting was held at 9 Conduit Street, Regent Street, London, December 5th, 1867. Present: Mrs Manning (in the Chair), Rev. Sedley Taylor, H. R. Tomkinson Esq., Miss Davies (secretary).

* *Emily Davies and Girton College*, p. 90; Ray Strachey, *The Cause*, p. 104.

Two Cambridge men, the first Mistress, and Miss Davies framed a few resolutions; a College for Women was to be formed – Cantabrigian; moderately Anglican (but with full freedom for dissent); feminine. The secretary was instructed to go ahead and form a larger committee, raise funds, arrange meetings.

Her manifesto, 'Some Account of a Proposed New College for Women', shows her at her best. It was read at the meeting of the Social Science Association in 1868.

She began by looking at the general issues (and the objections), and went on to describe the remedy and the plans to put it into being. Home education can never be of an advanced kind: everyone agrees that 'something is wanted for governesses'; and yet

> if neither governesses nor mother *know*, how can they teach? So long as education is not provided *for* them, how can it be provided *by* them?*

Examinations are not enough to raise the standard, for 'to suppose that examinations will do instead of teaching, is like supposing that given the assaying process, you can make a sovereign without extracting gold from the ore . . . If we want education, we must first teach, then examine and certify.' Next, with the aid of some pointed and damning quotations from the Report of the Schools Commission, backed by confirmation of the school-mistresses themselves, she proved that the situation cannot be remedied solely by training given at schools. Thirdly, any system of public lectures benefits only the inhabitants of large towns and the universities – 'it cannot reach the great mass of young women of the upper class. It cannot do anything at all for the rural

* *Questions Relating to Women*, p. 87. Further references to this article are given in the text.

districts'. The universities are not fed by the great manufac-
turing towns, and the two thousand sisters of the two thousand undergraduates at Oxford and Cambridge are scattered
up and down in country houses and parsonages. 'The Hall
and the Rectory are centres of light for a whole parish. If
their light be darkness, how great is that darkness.' (p. 97)

And here comes the core of this argument, the wretched
life of young women condemned in effect to unemploy-
ment and permanent childishness by the social consequences
of the Industrial Revolution.

> Yes, domestic employments have gone out of fashion. But why
> have they gone out of fashion? There are two reasons; the
> increase of wealth, and the supply of domestic wants by
> machinery. There are more families of a condition to keep a
> staff of servants . . . 'Ready made' has taken the place of
> 'home made'. There is less work to do and there are more
> servants to do it. (p. 98)

Idleness, however, is not fashionable and 'the young lady of
the world is universally condemned . . . We are all agreed
that the sooner she is abolished the better.'

> But what are we to have in her place? That is the question . . .
> Not . . . the pale-faced student poring over miserable books.
> We want the healthy, happy, dutiful English woman; and we
> are persuaded that if women take to College, and examinations,
> and diplomas, and the rest, they will be unhealthly, unhappy,
> undutiful, and worst of all – American. (p. 99)

This last ironic broadside, it may be assumed, does not refer
to the Declaration of Independence but to co-educational
schools (and maybe the foundation, in 1865, of Vassar
College).

Miss Davies pleaded that she was not trying to give young

women 'an unusual quantity of information' (this was good Queen's College doctrine!):

> So long as education is treated only as a means of getting on in the world, nothing is easier to show than that the women for whom the getting on has been done by other people do not want it . . . . The object of the new College is not to enable women to make money, though that may probably be among the results indirectly attained. . . . It will not be directed towards changing the occupations of women, but rather towards securing that whatever they do shall be done well.

It is only a temporary stage in 'the education of life'. But girls are expected to be grown up at eighteen; and then in mature life the older woman suffers from want of training, and has to acquire what should have come to her as part of her education. (p. 102)

These sentiments, in more impassioned and less orderly style, had been those of Florence Nightingale in her terrifying and tragic fragment *Cassandra*.

> What form do the Chinese feet assume when denied their proper development?
> Give us back our suffering, we cry to Heaven in our hearts – suffering rather than indifferentism; for out of nothing comes nothing. But out of suffering may come the cure. Better have pain than paralysis. A hundred struggle and drown in the breakers. One discovers the new world.*

Miss Davies's last point is the defence of the married woman's right to education:

> It is, in fact, often taken for granted that though for women who have only themselves to think of, it may be a good thing

* Ray Strachey, *The Cause*, pp. 396, 398.

to have some intellectual resources, for *mothers* there is nothing like good sound ignorance . . . Englishmen of the present day are such a nervously excitable race, that the only chance for their descendants is to keep the mothers in a state of coma.

The theory that starving the brain is the way to keep it healthy is not supported by medical testimony.

This apprehension, a regular one among all who felt protective towards women, is rebutted by quoting Dr Maudsley – who, alas, was later to desert the cause. For six years later, the great psychiatrist wrote to the *Fortnightly Review* in support of a separate type of education for women; he instanced as a bad example the United States of America where girls received the same education as boys, and became (so he said) physically unfit for their duties as women. Elizabeth Garrett was at once told off to deal with the perfidious Maudsley and did so in the next number of the *Review*:

> The school-mistresses who asked that girls might share in the Oxford and Cambridge Local Examinations were also the first to introduce gymnastics, active games, daily baths, and *many* other hygienic reforms.★

She spoke with authority; for when, after the Education Act of 1870, the London School Boards were formed, two women only were elected; for Greenwich Miss Emily Davies, and for Marylebone – by 47,000, a thumping majority – Miss Garrett.

And when the College was formed, Miss Garrett was to come down and instruct students in the use of the gymnasium, which they did not understand, although one could 'do the trapeze'.†

★ *Emily Davies and Girton College*, pp. 290–92.
† MSS letters to Mme Bodichon at Girton College, dated 20 November, 1867 and 11 October, 1869.

Benslow House, Hitchin. The College for Women, 1869–1873

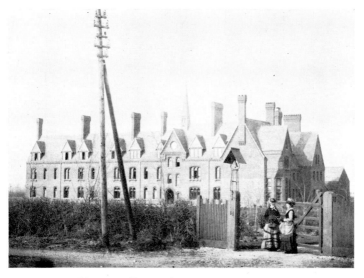

Girton College. The first buildings, 1874

ELIZABETH GARRETT, EMILY DAVIES

III

An unsuccessful attempt had been made in 1862 to open the examinations of London University to women, in order that Miss Garrett might sit them; Miss Davies knew that 'we must begin at the top' (this too was Miss Garrett's policy), so she took a steady aim at the impossible, and set her plans towards Cambridge.

In the sixties, Oxford and Cambridge, though the Royal Commission of 1850 brought about many improvements, were still semi-reformed institutions, where standards of teaching were in process of being raised by vigorous movements from within.[*] They had strict requirements of residence and very little else; less than half the young men who went up took a degree in honours. Leslie Stephen's *Sketches from Cambridge*, published in 1865, told the tale of the Greek Testament class; 'Hello! Easy all! hard word there. Smith, what does it mean?' 'I don't know' says Smith. 'No more don't I; paddle on, all!' But the influence of Seeley, who in 1869 became Regius Professor of History, of Henry Sidgwick and Mather Jackson brought about a reform in college teaching.

Youthful teachers at Cambridge, who were bent on reforming their own syllabus, would have preferred women to start with something better and different; on the other hand, some were content to aim at standards less ambitious than the Tripos and to work through external lectures, with examinations attached to them. In 1866 London, and 1869, Cambridge, established special sets of advanced examinations for ladies.

[*] See Sheldon Rothblatt, *The Revolution of The Dons*, 1968.

Miss Davies was an out-and-outer. There could be no 'easy second best'; and to ensure standards, at first it was necessary to insist on a demonstration of equality. On these principles she formed her London and Cambridge committees. She had the advice and help of some of the best Cambridge men – Henry Liveing, Henry Sidgwick, Sedley Taylor, John Seeley, E. C. Clarke, James Stuart, John Venn, and F. J. A. Hort all promised to assist with lecturing or advising.

'I do not feel at all humble about our teachers,' wrote Miss Davies. 'Those we have in view at present are all of the first rank, and I do not feel inclined to look lower.'*

But the lady to whom this observation was addressed was herself too unconventional to appear on the Executive Committee. A first cousin of Florence Nightingale, Barbara Leigh Smith, later became a co-founder; her qualities were exactly complementary to those of Emily Davies.†

Like Miss Garrett, Barbara Leigh Smith was the daughter of a wealthy man who was prepared to give her independence; he actually settled £300 a year on his daughter. She became an artist – learning drawing at the newly founded Bedford College, for her family were Unitarians like its foundress, but also espoused the woman's cause in all its forms. In her school, boys and girls learnt together without creed, without punishments, without uniforms. Generous, impulsive, and vividly lovely, with a tall figure, blue eyes and red-gold hair, she became the centre of movements for employment of women, for reform of marriage laws, and preached a crusade in *The Englishwoman's Journal*, which she

* *Emily Davies and Girton College*, p. 207.

† D. G. Rossetti had been attracted by her, and described her to a friend as 'having plenty of fair hair, fat, and "tin", and readiness to climb a mountain in breeches or ford a river without them.' (W. Graeme Robertson, *When Time Was*, 1931.)

helped to found. Her *Woman's Work*, 1857, remains the best account of the early movement. Direct work was rather cut short when in this same year – 1857 – she married a French doctor Eugène Bodichon; but they made a tour of North America, especially the slave states, whence Barbara returned a passionate abolitionist and converted to American school methods.

One of Mme Bodichon's intimate friends was George Eliot, who used her as the model for Romola. (Barbara had been the first to recognise the author of *Adam Bede*, and had written warmly.) It took some courage to call on 'Mrs Lewes' to discuss the college, but an influential Quakeress assured Emily Davies that it would be proper to do so, though not to meet other people at the house. The Leweses agreed that 'the same platform as Cambridge' about religious matters was desirable and

> she (Mrs Lewes) also strongly approves of having women only as resident authorities, and thought that people who recommended a man and his wife could not have much knowledge of life . . . She says the principles of Hygiene are so few and so simple that anybody could learn them . . . Mr Lewes took exactly the same view. He thought it desirable to have some teaching of the laws of life, but that, he said, would come under Zoology.*

Fifty pounds was subscribed 'from the author of *Romola*' – whose name naturally could not be used – but Emily Davies, while later assuring Anna Richardson of her reverence for 'Mrs Lewes', did not feel able to tell her the substance of the discussion.

Miss Davies collected on her Committee a number of

* Quoted from MS letter from E.D. to Mme Bodichon dated 20 November 1867, now at Girton College.

men concerned with education, some bishops and deans, Lady Augusta Stanley (who had been in the Queen's household), Mrs Gurney, wife of the Recorder of London, and Louisa Goldsmid, the wife of the first member of the Hebrew community to become a barrister and M.P

Another ultimate co-founder could not join the committee at this time. Lady Stanley of Alderley, whom Miss Davies met in connexion with the suffrage movement, was put by her at the top of the list of her committee, but did not join because 'it is not liked for my name to appear before the public'. Miss Davies was worried about her Cambridge Committee because 'they are all young men', and thought 'if we could get a few more old ladies like Lady Stanley of Alderley who has six grown-up daughters and a multitude of grandchildren, they might counterbalance the levity of young Cambridge'.* After her husband's death, Lady Stanley was able to become open in her support and even acted as Mistress of the College for a short time; a daughter and granddaughter followed her in support and membership; her grandson, Bertrand Russell, after a spirited and emancipated wooing of Dora Black, a Research Fellow of the College, married her.† But that was more than half a century later.

Rebuffs continued also. Miss Christina Rossetti declined to assist because the College was not to be Catholic ('Anglo-Catholic' was Miss Davies's chilly annotation). That other pillar of the Church, Miss Charlotte M. Yonge, wrote on black-edged paper:

I am obliged to you for your letter respecting the proposed college for ladies, but as I have decided objections to bringing large numbers of girls together and think home education under the inspection or encouragement of sensible fathers or voluntarily

* *Emily Davies and Girton College*, p. 165.
† *The Autobiography of Bertrand Russell*, vol. II, 1968, Ch. 2.

undertaken by the girls themselves is far more valuable both intellectually and morally than any external education I am afraid I cannot assist you.

I feel with regret that female education is deficient in tone and manner, if in nothing else. Superior women will always teach themselves and inferior women will never learn enough for more than home life.★

Mrs Gatty, authoress of *Parables from Nature* and editress of *Aunt Judy's Magazine*, also drew back in disapprobation.

Emulating St Paul in being all things to all men (it encouraged her to think how 'worried' and nervous he was about his Missions), Miss Davies had explained that a certain number of options would be allowed, and that 'no subject which competent authorities regard as fit for the higher education of an English lady will be excluded' but that it was intended as far as possible to be officially connected with Cambridge. 'The College is intended to be a dependency, a living branch of Cambridge. It will aim at no higher position than, say, that of Trinity College.' 'Such a degree of humility', commented *The Times*, 'will not be considered excessive.'

To emulate Trinity College there remained the trifling matter of finance. Miss Davies had boldly launched a campaign for £30,000. Mr Tomkinson, with equal boldness, fixed the fees at a hundred guineas a year. The little circle of well-wishers gave generously, but £2,000 was all that could be collected and half of this came from Barbara Bodichon. The invaluable Mr Tomkinson told Miss Davies what to do with subscriptions. 'I am so much obliged to you for instructing me about business,' she wrote; 'I feel very ignorant about it and it would be disastrous to be making mistakes.'

★ This letter is preserved at Girton College.

From 1869 to 1875, in addition to acting as Conciliator-general, he became the treasurer. Miss Garrett promised to pay in instalments though 'always expecting that patients will suddenly come to an end – all get well at once – or something equally calamitous as this'.

The pleasant house at Hitchin was hired, and furnished in a somewhat Spartan fashion; according to Miss Lloyd 'our beds are to be as small as possible, we are not to be allowed dressing-tables, but a looking-glass large enough to see the tip of the nose is to be placed somewhere on the walls; the carpet is to be a small piece in the middle of the room, in the centre of which a student's table consisting of ten drawers is to be placed'. This last was clearly to be the most important object of furniture. Subsequently the beds were found to be short and the sheets narrow, so that tall young women suffered great discomfort; yet in a year's time Anna Lloyd could write from her 'large armchair by the fire':

It looks rather pretty, my room by firelight, with the crimson curtains only half drawn, and the moon making a grey light outside in which the almost leafless trees are dark and still, and by contrast the firelight glances warmly on the small table with its vase of flowers and the pictures and statuettes . . . *

A room of one's own, and a year walking and talking about William Morris and the Pre-Raphaelites round the lanes of Hertfordshire had done much for the little Quakeress from the Midland town; this, no less than her Classics and Mathematics, was the higher education.

Food was simple; 'We have good plain food, milk, bread, beef and butter and it disappears very fast,' wrote Emily Davies; but she would not allow eggs or butter, only dripping, to be used in the puddings. Before long, there were

* *Anna Lloyd*, p. 69.

26

grumbles. More dangerous still, cheap candles only were issued. Miss Davies expected heroic standards and tough frames. In winter, one young woman went round wrapped in a railway rug. At the same time academic formality was observed, with a high table for two, and a commoners' table for the five students: 'We might have been fifty undergraduates, instead of five harmless young women,' as Louisa Lumsden observed; and later she revealed that this basement room (the dining-room of the house served as library) was shared with black beetles.* For Miss Davies, however, all was splendid. 'Photographs of the College are already on sale in this town,' she told Mme Bodichon on 11 October.†

The students were full of a sense of responsibility, and most anxious not to be treated as schoolgirls; but did the members of the High Table ever have to supervise the pudding before rustling in to preside over the meal?

When in 1871 the move to Girton was planned, a wide campaign and a very determined struggle raised only about £3,000; the new building was estimated to cost about £7,800 and all the original subscriptions had been spent on furnishings at Hitchin, including a 'Tin Tabernacle' in the garden, where some of the students lived. So that by the advice of Sir Francis Goldsmid, the College borrowed on the security of a number of friends, who acted as guarantors. For this reason it was incorporated under the Board of Trade, a form of association that continued till 1924.

The new buildings were put up on a generous scale, with two rooms for each student (except in the attics). Miss Davies wanted them to be 'as beautiful as the Assize Courts at Manchester' and so Alfred Waterhouse was chosen as the

---

* Louisa Innes Lumsden, *Yellow Leaves*, 1933, p. 47.
† MS. letter at Girton College.

architect; but funds limited the amount of Gothic ornamentation that could be permitted. The rather stark little block in the midst of empty fields was sparsely furnished, carpenters were still fixing the doors and the corridors filled with shavings, when fifteen students arrived in October 1873. The Mistress, Miss Emily Davies, came flying down the staircase wrapped in a little white shawl, to welcome them.*
By 1902, the building held 180 students; in little over thirty years, the College multiplied thirty-fold.

* *Emily Davies and Girton College*, p. 283. The description is by Dame Jane Frances Dove, founder of Wycombe Abbey School.

Chapter 2

TRIALS AND TEMPERAMENTS

ANNA LLOYD attempted to describe Emily Davies to her friend Mary Waterhouse:

*We always miss her very much. Her character is very indefinable. I cannot tell what makes its charm exactly. I think she has very quick perceptions joined with good sense and sympathy underneath, very largely developed, yet seldom brought to the surface. After all, I believe it is this sympathy that causes her influence, united with a naturally clever mind. She does not seem to make the slightest effort to be anything or do anything great or just. She never expresses fine moral sentiments about unselfishness or service, yet she is unselfish and ministers to others. I feel there is much to be learnt from her example.**

The stern North country environment in which she had been reared had tempered Miss Davies's Welsh blood without softening her pointed features or nervous staccato speech. Her successor in the mistress-ship spoke of her as a 'stout-hearted general', but to Barbara Bodichon she could recall something of their common ordeals in the heartbreaking and unsuccessful campaign of 1871:

. . . altogether I felt there was a great deal more sympathy than that dreadful day when you and I sat with all their stony faces before us and failed to move them at all.

[She hated] . . .

the perpetual necessity of asking people to do something which

* *Anna Lloyd, p. 64.*

29

*they [do not] care for, and will only do, if at all, out of good nature ... and in most cases, I am not likely to have an opportunity of making any return for the good nature. It is a pull upon one's pride and it takes a great deal of care for a thing to wind one up to doing it. However, it must be done, and I go through a certain amount of hair-shirt every day.**

A few months later she went as far as to confess to Henry Tomkinson:

It has often occurred to me if I were dead or in some way entirely prevented from doing anything here, it might be the best solution of our difficulties. If that is true, the wise thing would be for me to keep away.

Mr Tomkinson could speak plainly to her; he accused her of dividing everyone into friends and enemies and denouncing the second. She replied:

I am afraid that I feel very vindictive generally. It is the fierceness of fear. If I felt more confident, I might perhaps be more amiable.†

In turn, she spoke with sharpness to Elizabeth Garrett who, with her 47,000 votes for election to the School Board, felt she was qualified to chair the meeting. This was 'cheeky' and 'it is true that your jokes are many and reckless. They do more harm than you know'. Elizabeth showed the letter to her fiancé, with the comment: 'I do not mind a little North East wind'.‡

Open differences with students and lecturers at the college developed early, and the first student to become a lecturer herself, Dame Louisa Lumsden, resigned her post after one

* *Emily Davies and Girton College*, p. 262.
† Ibid, p. 278.
‡ Jo Manton, *Elizabeth Garrett Anderson*, p. 209.

such difference. To the end of Dame Louisa's life the bitterness remained; she felt 'the student was a mere cog in the wheel of her [Emily Davies's] great scheme. There was a fine element in this, a total indifference to popularity but . . . it was plain we counted for little or nothing, except as we furthered her plans.'* Even Mme Bodichon wrote to her friend Sarah Marks:

> *I think we all felt the want in Miss Davies of genial wisdom and influence . . . she who has an immense love of justice for women would die to give young women what she never had herself in early life, ah, die to get it for them, though she might hate every individual.*

The two issues on which Miss Davies remained utterly unpersuadable were that young women must follow exactly the same course as was required for Cambridge undergraduates, and that they must not reside in Cambridge itself. Both were defended by 'the fierceness of fear'; for these principles she would sacrifice opportunities, friendships, would even risk the shipwreck of her whole scheme. On the first issue she clashed with students of the College and Cambridge dons, but she maintained her point; and in later years even Louisa Lumsden conceded that she was right.

One of the chief difficulties of the early days at Hitchin was that students were expected to prepare for the elementary 'Little-Go', or Previous Examination, at the same time as they worked for the Tripos or Final Examination. The Little-Go had just been reformed and included Additional Mathematics and other severities, of which nearly all were woefully ignorant. The students felt it very hard and hampering to pursue these studies almost to the last moment along with their higher work. Not that the Cambridge

* *Girton College*, p. 37.

syllabus itself could be considered ideal – many of the teachers thought it very bad, and even Mme Bodichon did not think as well of it as Emily Davies – so that some of the youthful and enthusiastic young gentlemen who came out to Hitchin were more concerned to advance the general culture of the young ladies than to coach for examinations. They wanted to broaden their pupil's minds – or had little notion of strict relevance in any case. The students were driven to protest, and in fact 'shunted' two eminent persons, as Louisa Lumsden put it – Professor Seeley, who as the author of *Ecce Homo* was very influential; but he lectured on *Lycidas*, and set students to write verses. The Rev. Mr Hort also insisted on talking about *Acts*, when the book prescribed was *Luke*. Seeley was extremely angry, and withdrew his support, for he had already had many differences with Miss Davies about sending in her students for the new Cambridge Higher Examination for women.

This had been instituted in the very year the College opened, and was eventually to develop into the Higher Locals. The great northern cities began lecture courses at which ladies could prepare for the Higher Examination, Hundreds could benefit. The movement in the North was led by Anne Jemima Clough, but there were some who felt that even at Cambridge the course offered better chances to the individual student, badly prepared as many of them were, than Degree examinations; and it attracted the Cambridge Ladies.

Miss Davies had already fought this principle of separate standards for women at London, where it had been introduced three years before; she had written with extreme heat, for it undermined both the existing arrangement with the Cambridge Local Examinations and her plans for a Women's College.

I am afraid the people who are interested in improving the education of women are a thankless crew . . . we should not like to seem ungrateful. We are really obliged to Convocation for their kind intention in offering us a serpent when we asked for a fish, though we cannot pretend to believe that serpents are better for us.*

When she was further challenged, she declared: 'I am sorry to say my stock of beliefs is but small, but on this point I have no doubt whatever – I mean as to the general principle': yet she thought this wicked London examination might prove a useful entrance test for her college. Now when the 'serpent' reared its head at Cambridge too she wrote passionately to Anna Richardson about 'the Liverpool faction':

Miss Clough and her section don't want Degrees . . . Now, however, the question is being put; Do practical, thoughtful and working women want Degrees and a common standard or is it only the clamour of a few fanatics and women's rights people?†

Even Mr Tomkinson betrayed her by thinking that the College might be examined independently by members of London, Oxford and Cambridge Universities.

Miss Davies would allow the students at Hitchin to have nothing to do with any such outrageous compromise as these special examinations. The most she would concede was that students who worked for the Ordinary Degree might have some leisure to study extra-curricular subjects, such as French, History and Political Institutions; and so could be given a College Certificate. But in fact the prestige of the Tripos quickly won the students, and the College

* *Emily Davies and Girton College*, p. 103.
† Ibid, p. 191.

Certificate became simply a way of showing that they had followed the full Cambridge course.

Sidgwick tried hard to be conciliatory, but 'Miss Davies keeps perplexing me', he admitted, and even 'Emily Davies ... weighs on my soul'; still, he had felt when he first started the ladies' lectures in 1869 that 'many experiments are necessary before the exact form which the higher education of women ought to take can be determined'.*

Miss Davies kept absolute standards; for her 'Different means lower'. After one college had shown that men's standards could be attained, it was possible and less damaging for its successors to adopt more pragmatic and less inhuman programmes. Miss Davies had to be a perfectionist, because the prejudice and assumption of the inherent inferiority of women's intellectual capacity must be exposed in an unambiguous fashion. Admission to degrees, good or bad, was the intellectual equivalent of the Vote. Justice must be done and must be seen to be done.

She felt this because she saw the educational issue within the larger matter of women's suffrage and other aspects of the Cause, whereas her Cambridge supporters saw it within the orbit of their own attempts to reform the Cambridge syllabus, about which they knew much more than she did. But it may be that the need for an absolute standard is felt by exceptional women in each generation.

A second reason was that Miss Davies had intimately shared Miss Garrett's struggle to enter the medical profession – one in which compromise would have been impossible since the Act of 1858 and the G.M.C.'s regulations. In practice Miss Garrett 'qualified' by becoming a member of the Society of Apothecaries – after she had refused her father's offer to endow a 'Female Medical College', had studied in

* A. S. and E. M. S., *Henry Sidgwick, A Memoir*, pp. 255–6, p. 226.

Edinburgh, had walked the wards, and faced a campaign of insult; when she *was* examined, she sometimes did better than anybody else. Miss Davies had learnt in this hard school with her friend.

The third and perhaps the most compelling reason, though not openly produced by Miss Davies, was the hybrid development at the two London colleges, Queen's College and Bedford College. In her friendship with F. D. Maurice, Emily Davies was closely linked to Queen's College; but his noble design of a liberal education – 'The teachers of a school may aim merely to impart information; the teachers of a college must lead their pupils to the apprehension of principles' – had not been measured against definite external standards, but rather had precluded them. In 1863 Miss Davies had been ready to hail Queen's College as a place where the London Pass Degree might be acquired★; in 1866, despairing of London University she had applied for the secretaryship of Queen's College herself, in the hope that she might get it affiliated to Cambridge. Lady Stanley of Alderley was one of the Lady Visitors at Queen's; in 1872 Miss Davies's brother Llewelyn became Principal, a position he held for some years, and her niece was a pupil there. But in the manifesto 'Some Account of a proposed New College for Women' (1868) Miss Davies quotes the Assistant Commissioner for London District in his report to the Schools Inquiry Commission as saying he had been unable to discover anywhere in London that conducted the Higher Education for girls 'in such a regular and systematic way that it could be recognised by the Commission'. Miss Davies added: 'If such an institution is not to be found in London, it certainly will not be found anywhere else in England.'†

★ *Questions Relating to Women*, p. 55.
† Ibid, p. 85.

Both Queen's College and Bedford College included flourishing girls' schools as part of the establishment, and though their origins had been similar, their ways diverged only by chance. Other colleges with mixed aims were Cheltenham – the training department moved to Oxford and became St. Hilda's – and Alexandra College, Dublin. Such establishments tended to become less and less systematic as training centres. Bedford College was reformed to become later a part of London University only by a *coup d'état*. Miss Smith of Oxford (a friend of Miss Davies) in 1864 virtually assumed control and closed the profitable school department. Emily Davies herself was a Lady Visitor at Bedford College, and inevitably her knowledge of what happened in London drove her to make a stand. Long after, she began an account of Women in the Universities with a reference to the London colleges as 'only in a general sense pioneers in the movement for opening universities to women. They were self-contained, and there is no evidence that they aimed at being attached to any university'.*

Cambridge men took a very different view, for they were engaged in quite a different battle to reform the syllabus, the lecture system and the religious tests.

All students and seven of the lecturers at Hitchin petitioned to be allowed to drop the Little-Go. 'The Hitchin girls have come over to take the Little-Go examination,' Henry Sidgwick told Myers on 18 September 1870. 'I am afraid that if they pass the examination, the Cambridge world will not be particularly impressed.'

This was the first term of their second year; the five who went to Cambridge were told on no account to reveal their dangerous mission. Louisa Lumsden was invited to lunch at Queens' and in old age recollected how

* Ibid, p. 160.

The Emily Davies
Court, Stanley
Library and Tower
Wing, 1887

The College, 1948

kind old Dr Phillips, the President, froze my blood by innocently remarking, in his slow and somewhat pompous fashion, that he believed there were 'some young women up in Cambridge to pass the Little-Go'.

'Yes,' said Mrs Latham coolly 'and there sits one.' I could have sunk under the table! Both Dr and Mrs Phillips were so kind, and they took the terrible revelation so calmly that I was soon reassured.'

At Jesus, however, she was warned not to divulge the secret or she might have been summarily ejected.

Later that year Henry Sidgwick, who had done so much for the College, took the bold step of hiring a house in Cambridge where ladies could reside to hear the special lectures for women, or take the special examination, regarding themselves as free from the need to conform. Miss Anne Jemima Clough came down from the North to preside over 74, Regent Street (the present Glengarry Hotel), which opened in the autumn of 1871; and one of Miss Davies's own students, Amy Bulley, left Hitchin to join the new establishment.

Miss Davies wrote to Henry Sidgwick 'affably':

> I am sure it is generous inconsistency and not cruel mockery on your part that makes you say you are willing to help us, when your scheme is the serpent that is gnawing at our vitals. It glides in everywhere.*

but she was thrown into such despair that she contemplated 'shutting up'. Over eighty people went to the special lectures, and to disregard the advice of such men as Sidgwick and Lightfoot made her appear merely 'to be grasping, without any real necessity, at the special privileges of men'.† (In fact,

---

* *Emily Davies and Girton College*, p. 255.
† Ibid, p. 256.

as late as 1920 there were still a few who wanted a separate university for women at Cambridge.)

She persisted; and as usual, carried her point. All her students passed the Little-Go; before the Hitchin years ended, and precisely when requirements stipulated they should do so, in the Lent Term of 1873, three sat the Tripos. Miss Woodhead took the mathematical papers, and a little later in the same term, Miss Cook and Miss Lumsden the classical papers. In February 1928 Louisa Lumsden was noted as being entitled by the university regulations to receive the M.A. titular degree.*

Henry Sidgwick, by developing Newnham College out of a programme based on the Higher Local Examinations, met the immediate needs of Cambridge; and soon, at Oxford, the higher education of women developed on similar lines. On the initiative of a small university group, in 1873 lectures were started there; the women's colleges began as hostels for ladies who came to follow this course, but 'Home Students' also persisted, and after 1893 they continued at Oxford as a non-collegiate society for a large number of women studying for degrees, till after the Second World War they were refounded as St Anne's College.

Emily Davies, by keeping to her principles, to some extent cut her College off from the academic sympathies of Cambridge. Girton had been founded by the 'women's rights people', not by internal efforts; it was a foreign graft. Sedley Taylor, Sidgwick himself and many others continued to help the College, which had been called into being by an ideal, not by 'practical people' – dons and school-mistresses. Miss Davies's was essentially a metropolitan and national project with a Cambridge connexion, whereas Sidgwick was

* *Yellow Leaves*, p. 58.

a Cambridge man; and the men who volunteered to serve on Miss Davies's Executive Committee in London could not have felt so close to the actual working as he.

It was only in 1909, when the Council moved to Cambridge, and permanent Cambridge Chairmen were elected, that Girton reaped the full advantage of such service as Sir Hugh Anderson, Arthur Berry, Archdeacon Cunningham and Peter Giles generously gave. The further moves towards full admission of women, in the Jubilee years of 1887 and 1897, were conducted largely by Sidgwick, though with full co-operation from Girton.

Miss Davies's second and equally rigid principle was that the College should not be in Cambridge. What would she have said of the new arrangement for Girton students to share lunch and the junior combination room privileges of Clare College! Miss Davies had been bred in the Rectory parlour; her views were nearer to Jane Austen's than to Charlotte Brontë's. Jane Austen wrote her novels at a table in the common sitting-room where she was open to every interruption – slipping them under a paper when guests appeared, or her attention was distracted in some other way. Before beginning the round of London entertainments in the Season, Florence Nightingale rose to study her blue books in her bedroom. In this light, perhaps, Emily Davies's insistence upon privacy and remoteness becomes more explicable. She wanted for her students not only a room of their own, but a room not too accessible to callers. In a lengthy letter to Henry Sidgwick she urged that if the College were in a town, the girls would have either to be restricted by regulations which would deprive them of independence and the discipline of deciding for themselves and acting on their own responsibility; or else they would continually have to be making choices to resist interruption. She traced the good health of students at Hitchin to the quiet regular unperplexed life.

> *And I cannot believe that we should sacrifice this at all to the same extent at two or three miles off as we should in the town itself. There would not be the morning calls, and the dropping in and the servants coming with notes to wait for an answer, and the general victimisation by idle ladies.**

Later still, when her college had been established for some time at Girton she wrote:

> *In a College, as is well known, a student has the inestimable advantage of being free from distraction. This great boon – the power of being alone – is perhaps the most precious distinctive feature of college life.†*

So, after many debates with the Cambridge Committee, and many arguments about the cost of transport, but with firm support from her brother and Mr Tomkinson she succeeded in the compromise of settling at Girton, two and a half miles from the centre of town. Here, Miss Davies hoped for country life and a large garden – though when it came to the point she always refused to spend money on the garden, which was left to the enterprise of her friends. But the students had not only a room of their own – for the most part, they had two. In 1879 a visiting American was as much impressed by the handsome accommodation as by the sparseness of the contents. Modesty, therefore, and the dangerous proximity of brothers (two had visited Hitchin) were not her only motives in seeking seclusion. To Anna Richardson Miss Davies could write more plainly:

> *Young women are kept away now by parental fears. Their*

* *Emily Davies and Girton College*, p. 253.
† *Questions Relating to Women*, p. 149. Written in 1878.

mothers would let them come if it were considered a creditable thing to do. Ladies of influence have to make other people think it creditable. It takes a good deal of courage to speak of the college as it is . . . If the more extreme course were adopted, a whole system of propaganda would be stopped. People like Mrs Gurney and Lady Augusta would feel their mouths closed. As Mrs Gurney said, they would be almost ashamed to speak of it.*

Those who would detect nothing more than accents of extreme prudery should remember that conditions in Cambridge were not those of an ordinary town. The Case of the Magdalene undergraduate had reached the London Press in 1859. A pro-proctor, having caught the young man in a brothel, brought him before the Vice Chancellor's Court, which had newly been given powers to try 'grave offences', whereas previously such matters had been dealt with by the colleges, who had imposed only 'the same penalty as would be inflicted on one who had failed to attend lectures regularly'. The Vice Chancellor thought this offence not grave enough to require more than 'admonition', and wrote to the Senior Proctor saying 'none but aggravated cases of delinquency' should be referred to his Court. Loud public argument and some resignations ensued.

Next year, an even greater scandal came; the Vice Chancellor was sued in the Common Pleas by a young woman whom he had imprisoned in the Spinning House, the special university prison for prostitutes, and for women suspected of being prostitutes. She had been taken from an omnibus which, with a party of undergraduates and a small band, was making for Great Shelford, where supper and breakfast had been ordered; and she had with her a 14-year-old sister. The girls protested they were virtuous seamstresses.

* *Emily Davies and Girton College, p. 248.*

41

Emma Kempe was given her verdict, but it was also made clear that the Vice Chancellor was entitled to his special Court and his special prison (which stood on the site of the modern Police Station, St Andrew's Street).*

So that eleven years later, the ladies in Mr Sidgwick's hostel, backing on Parker's Piece, were carefully safeguarded by strict chaperon rules (the unworldly philosopher had placed it near to the Spinning House, and was it not on Parker's Piece that Emma Kempe had been arrested?). The house was 'dark', the neighbourhood noisy; the girls had no garden, and could not enjoy a room of their own. Next year, at Merton Hall, things greatly improved. But even so, young Mr Sidgwick (he was only 33) found his charges resented the middle-aged Miss Clough's concern for the proprieties; and would not take guidance. He admitted, 'They will not submit to maternal government.'† Regulations therefore would have to be devised.

It is hardly necessary to look a little further at the 'Death Riots' of 1875 or the increasing numbers consigned to the Spinning House, which remained till 1894; its abolition was attacked in Parliament because of the 'large numbers of young women studying at Girton and Newnham' who, it was thought, would be better protected by University regulation of morals than if this were left to the town police.

When I was an undergraduate there was a story of the proctor stopping a man asking to be introduced to the lady he was escorting. 'My sister' was the bland reply. 'Young man, don't you know that she is one of the most notorious women in Cambridge?' asked the Proctor, only to be answered, 'Yes, sir; mother's very worried about it.'

* D. A. Winstanley, *Later Victorian Cambridge*, Chapter IV.
† E. A. Hamilton, *Newnham, an informal Biography*, 1936, pp. 99–100.

Miss Davies was always ready to sing the praises of seclusion and privacy; but the students grew heartily to dislike the isolation of Hitchin, and found the régime at Girton lonely too, when contrasted with the happier lot of Newnhamites. Miis Lumsden heard enviously of their 'meeting interesting people – Mr Gladstone and others'.

Even the little amusements they devised for themselves were apt to bring trouble. Miss Lumsden could 'do the trapeze' and was good at games; 'she is a jewel', wrote Miss Davies.★ The students swam – and Miss Gibson rescued Miss Lumsden from drowning. They played croquet; Mr Tomkinson taught them fives. They then tried to play football, but Miss Davics forbadc it. Thcy wcrc drivcn to running up the hill to watch the Edinburgh express slip its coach – to tramp long country walks in search of wild flowers and trudge home singing the College Songs they had composed, often to airs military and defiant – a scene which Miss Davies would not have tolerated. The great and explosive issue, however, turned out to be amateur theatricals, over which Miss Davies took up an attitude that the authoress of *Mansfield Park* would have found extremely proper, but which very nearly closed the College.

In March 1871 the 'College Five' as the students called their club, asked Miss Davies and the classical tutor Miss Wedgwood to witness a rehearsal – a passage from *Atalanta in Calydon*, followed by 'some scenes between Benedick and Beatrice, and then Olivia and Malvolio and the Page'. 'What seems to us seriously objectionable,' Miss Davies told Mr Tomkinson, preparing to summon a Committee, 'was the taking male parts and dressing accordingly' (she revealed that this was close-fitting). Everyone disapproved; 'Russell says,' wrote Mrs Gurney, 'that in his Cambridge days this

★ MS. letter at Girton College, 11 October 1869.

43

very thing was put a stop to'; even George Eliot, consulted by Mme Bodichon, expressed disapprobation. Miss Lumsden defiantly said she had done the same thing at home, and Mme Bodichon, who as a theatre-goer was called in to remonstrate, 'had never met such a spirit of revolt and self-confidence'. Some students, who felt their freedom and responsibility were at stake, had thoughts of resigning; but eventually they were persuaded to drop their plans.

'Mrs Austin [the Mistress] thinks . . . this trouble is partly due to too much reading of *The Earthly Paradise*,' lamented Miss Davies. 'It is a sort of mixed notion of being artistic and worshipping Nature.'

While in relation to its standards and its organisation, Miss Davies had the very clearest views about the College, she herself had no experience of working for an examination of any kind; and she had no notion of the self-governing nature of a college. On both these matters she came into conflict with the undergraduates, the lecturers and a growing body of certificated students. On the second she was ultimately defeated.

The young women worked at full stretch, helping one another, to make up their appalling deficiences. Lectures at Hitchin were governed neither by their needs nor the lecturer's wishes but by the time of the trains. Louisa Lumsden described the last Long Vacation before her Tripos:

All through my last Long Vacation I coached Miss Dove for her Little-Go by correspondence. That last vacation was a horror – I do not like to think of it even now. I left home to gain complete freedom from social interruption, and lived for some weeks alone in lodgings in St Andrews, struggling against persistent headaches. Miss Cook at that time nearly threw the whole thing up, but I managed to persuade her to stick to our attempt.*

Miss Woodhead, who at 18 had been the youngest entrant to the College, was the first to sit her mathematical papers, after ten terms, the regulation time. She passed with the Senior Optimes. Later that term, Miss Lumsden and Miss Cook drove with Miss Davies to the University Arms Hotel and sat waiting for the first classics paper, which did not arrive. Miss Davies, knitting away steadily by the fire, hid her fears, for one of the examiners had threatened that he would not help them. All her life, Miss Lumsden could recall the click of the needles. When at last the messenger came, Miss Lumsden's nerve was shattered; 'it settled my class, a Third', she observed. Miss Cook took things more coolly (and achieved a Second Class) but as both sat afterwards looking on the Cam from King's Bridge, they felt that 'if the water had not been so muddy, one plunge might have ended all'. To their friends they seemed flippant, 'but it was the flippancy of despair'.

When the news of success reached Hitchin there were wild scenes indeed. Three flags were run up on the roof, and the alarm bell rung so loudly by the students that they called out the Hitchin Fire Brigade.

And yet when the committee invited the two classics to meet them in London, and Miss Cook mistook the address and did not come, Miss Lumsden was long kept waiting in an anteroom and was then told that they could not receive her without Miss Cook. Mme Bodichon, who had volunteered for the difficult task of telling Miss Lumsden, brought a

* *Yellow Leaves*, p. 53.

bouquet, her own offering. Miss Lumsden stalked out and threw the flowers in the gutter. When a second invitation came, she simply ignored it, not giving the committee even the refusal they had certainly earned. Miss Lumsden at this time was 32 years of age, Miss Cook just 25.[*]

In the May term, Miss Lumsden returned as Classical Tutor; she found the students overworking, in need of sympathy and even, from time to time, of a little home nursing. She became their spokesman. They had already revolted *en masse* and sent a petition to be let off Little-Go, as were Mr Sidgwick's students; seven of the college lecturers supported them. In fact everyone at Cambridge was agreed. Miss Davies was adamant. She fiercely defended the Little-Go. Eventually Miss Lumsden's name was put forward for the Executive Committee, and supported by Mme Bodichon and others; Miss Davies again opposed this proposal, and so Miss Lumsden resigned. A short period at Cheltenham Ladies' College prepared her for her great work as the first headmistress of St Leonards School, St Andrews: Miss Dove, who followed her there, later founded Wycombe Abbey.

The triumph of the three 'Girton Pioneers' – who were really the Hitchin Pioneers – is celebrated in the most famous of the Girton College Songs, sung to the tune of 'The British Grenadiers' and always given with applause. It begins bravely 'Some talk of Senior Wranglers and some of Double Firsts' but the next verse betrays anxiety behind the bravado:

> *Whenever we go forward*
> *A hard exam to try,*
> *Their memory goes before us*
> *To raise our courage high.*

[*] Ibid, pp. 57–8.

In asserting that they 'knew no doubts or fears' the singers did less than justice to the tremulous determination of

> *Woodhead, Cook and Lumsden,*
> *The Girton Pioneers.*

Rachel Cook, who accompanied Louisa Lumsden, was a fellow Highlander, a tall dark, willowy beauty with the melancholy air of one of Rossetti's nymphs, classical features and graceful movements. Everyone was charmed by her; George Eliot called her sylphlike. Within a year she had married C. P. Scott of the *Manchester Guardian*, and devoted herself to getting lectures arranged at Owens College. In 1880, when the Victoria University of Manchester was founded and opened to women, she forwarded this work too.

Sarah Woodhead, the tall athletic young Quakeress (who when at Hitchin declared that without rising from her chair in the Tin Tabernacle she could either poke the fire or open the door of her room) joined Rachel Scott at Manchester as mathematics mistress at the High School, and continued with school work after marrying C. G. B. Corbett. Of the other College Five, Emily Gibson – who had taken a leading part in the amateur theatricals – lured away from mathematics by the charms of Political Economy, was thrilled to find she was to be examined by 'my saint and hero, the author of *The Subjection of Women*' J. S. Mill. She refused her elementary revision and never sat her Tripos; Within a year she had married the brother of the fifth student, Isabella Townshend; afterwards through Rachel Scott she also became associated with the *Manchester Guardian*. Mrs Townshend is the only one of the Girton Pioneers I ever met, when as an exquisitely pretty white-haired old lady of 84 she came to an old students' session, and talked of her work for women's suffrage.

'I will give you a useful hint, my dears,' she said: 'If ever you have to go to prison, remember two things; take a change of linen, so they will know you are a lady; and say you are a vegetarian, the food is better if you do.' She had suffered fourteen days' imprisonment for the Cause.

Her future sister-in-law, Isabella Townshend, whose devotion to art fired both Emily Gibson and Anna Lloyd, worked only in fits and starts, gave up the Tripos and retired to Italy as a painter. According to Emily Gibson she systematically practised a sweet disorder, which cannot have been congenial to authority.

Before the students left Hitchin, two other notable women appeared: pretty Eliza Baker, from the North London Collegiate School, who insisted on doing Political Economy and History (Miss Davies thought everything except Classics and Mathematics a soft option). She married John Lewis of the John Lewis Partnership. Constance Louisa Maynard, was the first Girtonian to take the Moral Science Tripos; and with Miss Lumsden and Miss Welsh (a future Mistress) she exerted a great influence on the other students, which in her case was a religious one. She became the first Mistress of Westfield College, London, having found Girton distressingly 'Pagan'.

Religious affiliations and practice were a burning question at Cambridge in the sixties. Dissenters were first admitted to degrees in 1856, but senior offices were not open.

From 1862 to 1871 a series of Parliamentary Bills attempted to abolish religious tests. In the university the warfare was almost incessant; the *status quo* was sustained, though supported only by a minority. Sidgwick was an ardent supporter of abolition, and in 1869 he resigned his Trinity Fellowship in protest. Eventually, while morning and evening prayers were stipulated to be held in colleges, the general requirements were much relaxed.* Miss Davies, as a daughter of the Rectory and a friend of F. D. Maurice, took a liberal view but required some religious observance (not obligatory), and that it should eventually be written into the Articles of Association. By this she lost supporters; Mrs Garrett Anderson's husband and John Stuart Mill withdrew their offer of subscriptions. Henry Fawcett, Mrs Garrett Anderson's brother-in-law, was one of the ardent campaigners, and a prop of Sidgwick's foundation at Newnham, which was uncommitted to any religious view. So, although the foundation at Girton had the support of Quakers, Unitarians and Hebrews, and although there were no restrictions of personal freedom, for a time Cambridge undergraduates would come out to Girton in the hopes of seeing the young ladies marched to church in a crocodile. However, Miss Davies was pleased when some students volunteered to teach in the Sunday school, Miss Maynard's prayer-meeting became very powerful in moderating the influence of 'Pagans' and the record of Girton in the Mission Field soon became an outstanding one.

Just as at London, the religious differences had produced King's and University for men, Westfield and Bedford for Women, so at Oxford, Lady Margaret Hall and Somerville College were in 1879 founded within a few months of each other. But the distinction between Girton and Newnham, though partly a matter of religious affiliation, sprang chiefly from the early difference on academic requirements.

Girton students in the later seventies still expected to be outshone by Newnhamites who had not to face the Little-Go. This was the opinion of Sarah Marks, the beautiful Jewish girl whom George Eliot has drawn as Mira in *Daniel Deronda*, and who was destined to a brilliant career in science. Mme Bodichon, who had befriended Sarah in her early

* D. A. Winstanley, Chapter III.

struggles as a governess, looked on her almost as a daughter.* Miss Marks also told Mme Bodichon of a very gay ball held at the College, under the auspices of the new Mistress, Miss Bernard. At half-past one, the gentlemen were still begging for another dance and would not be denied.

In the early days of the College, a succession of Mistresses had appeared with bewildering speed;† then for three years, 1872–5, Miss Davies combined the offices of Mistress and secretary. Although objecting so strongly to anything savouring of a school, Miss Davies and her London Committee acted like a Board of Governors, and settled all matters of policy, leaving to the Mistress chiefly the duties of chaperon and housemistress. Neither the Mistress nor the lecturers were permitted to sit on this Committee – except the first Mistress, Mrs Manning, who had been there as of right. Of course Miss Davies, who was felt by all to be the real head, continued to sit while she held the office of Mistress. However, by 1875 she was extremely tired. Miss Bernard was secured by advertisement (before that, it had always been some volunteer from the little circle of friends.) The conditions of her appointment gave this lady charge of the students' work as well as of domestic arrangements.

Miss Bernard was elegant and distinguished; she had lived in India when her uncle Lord Lawrence was Viceroy so that the Cambridge Ladies, that close and jealous hierarchy, accorded her an honourable place in their midst. But her

* See H. Burton, *Barbara Bodichon* pp. 207–10.

† In an early stage, it had been apparently suggested that a man and wife might control the College, for after the visit to George Eliot, Miss Davies remarks, 'She also strongly appears to approve of having women only as resident authorities, and thought that people who recommended a man and his wife could not have much knowledge of life.' (MS. Letter of 20 March 1867, to Mme Bodichon, at Girton College.)

Later, 'a man and his wife' presided at Newnham – Professor and Mrs Sidgwick.

sense of the proprieties was even stronger than that of Miss Davies.

In May 1877 George Eliot wrote with restrained anger to Barbara Bodichon.

> *My Dear Barbara,*
> *I have been rather annoyed by Mr Lewes having told me yesterday that some unpleasantness had arisen between Miss Bernard and the students at Girton about the invitation sent to me . . . We are engaged to go to Mr Sidgwick on 21st . . . Mr Lewes says that you suggested my calling to see the College in the ordinary way but this affair with Miss Bernard makes me disinclined to appear there at all.*

So F. W. H. Myers might describe her visit:

> *I remember how at Cambridge, I walked with her in the Fellows' Garden at Trinity in Cambridge on an evening of rainy May and she . . . taking as her text the three words God, Immortality, Duty, pronounced with terrible conviction, how inconceivable was the* first, *how unbelievable the* second, *and yet how peremptory and absolute the* third *. . . I listened and might feel her grave, majestic countenance turned towards me like a sybil's in the gloom . . .*†

Jane Harrison might start up with delight as the wonderful figure entered her Newnham room; but at Girton (it was said) she drove in by the back drive only.

For a few years, after returning to London, Miss Davies, now 48 years of age, retired very largely from visits and societies; she took over the office of treasurer from Mr Tomkinson, and another secretary was appointed (a member of her own family circle). Later, she resumed this work, and

* *Letters of George Eliot*, ed. Gordon Haight, Vol VI, p. 374.
† Ibid, p. 380.

used to visit the College. To the students she had become someone remote; they now felt she treated them as members of a boarding-school; she moved about in a silent and alarming way (she was thought to wear bedroom slippers almost like Charlotte Brontë's schoolmistress spy, Mme Beck.) In Tripos Term of 1881 she found a young woman gazing from the corridor window at the sweet Maytime scene of the lawn, as she came in after a morning's work outside. 'Is this the way you do your work in the morning?' Miss Davies inquired; and many years later a very old lady recorded that moment, in which she felt a surge of resentment – 'even to ask such a question showed a lack of appreciation of the attitude of students'.*

However, another aspect of Miss Davies was shown when L. G. Montefiore wrote to the Bursar of Girton in 1961 about his mother, a former vice-mistress of the college; 'She had a good story about Miss Emily Davies. An undergraduate came to the Mistress and complained that she had never been kissed. Miss Davies replied: "My dear girl, what on earth have you done with your opportunities?"'

During the first years of its existence, the College was in no way recognised by the University of Cambridge. The Council of the Senate did not give permission for the students to sit examinations, but did not object to the examiners looking over the papers, in their private capacity. On each occasion therefore, both for Little-Go and Tripos, personal application had to be made; and sometimes there were sticky situations, but never an absolute breakdown. The tremulous fears of the young ladies and their teachers wore

* E. Reid Mumford, *Through Rose Coloured Spectacles*, 1952, p. 41.

Jane Catherine Gamble

The first five students at Hitchin, 1870

Left to right, standing: Isabella Townshend, Sarah Woodhead,
Emily Gibson. Seated: Rachel Cook, Louisa Lumsden

off, but were not quite extinguished. However, after London University opened its degrees in 1878, and the foundation of Manchester University in 1880 with admission of women, Henry Sidgwick lent his aid to a new move which had been started from outside by the success of a Girton student, Miss Charlotte Angas Scott, who in 1880 was bracketed (unofficially of course) with the eighth Wrangler in the Mathematical Tripos. More striking successes were to come, when at Newnham Miss Philippa Fawcett (niece of Elizabeth Garrett Anderson) was placed above the first Wrangler and at Girton Miss Agnata Frances Ramsay placed alone in the first division of the first class of the Classical Tripos. But these were in the future. Meanwhile on 24th February 1881 the Senate passed three Graces which allowed women officially to sit for the Tripos and Little-Go, while forbidding them to take the Pass Degree.*

'Scott of Girton,' cheered in the Senate House,† was at once elected to a Lectureship in Mathematics, but after four years, the first of the 'Brain Drain', she crossed the Atlantic to become professor of mathematics at the new ladies' college of Bryn Mawr, Pennsylvania. The public triumph is celebrated in another Girton College Song, to the tune of 'The Vicar of Bray':

When first a daring voice whispered, not void were women's brain pans,
The scornful critics all averred that notion was no sane man's.

* The arrangement, from Miss Davies's view, was not perfect; for she approved of the Pass Degree (which Sidgwick thought a bad thing); The Higher Locals were still a women's alternative to Little-Go, treated at Newnham as an end in themselves.

† Miss Scott was also noticed in *Punch* – 'The honour falls as pat as pleasant' – by contrast with an attack on the continued north country agitation for suffrage (See *Girton Girls and Lancashire Witches*, 7 February 1880).

Yet still in spite of sweeping blame and wholesale condemnation,
A women's college gained a name and local habitation,
When on that memorable day the Senate had assembled,
The crush was such that each M.A. for life and safety trembled.
They gave us rights where formerly we'd scarce been tolerated,
And thereon they no less than we should be congratulated.

In the chorus, however, this justifiable preening is replaced by mock-modesty:

> *Yet stranger sight for don or ped–*
> *Agogue was never seen, sir,*
> *Than Girton's buildings blushing red*
> *Behind a veil of green, sir.*

The gentlemen replied with a 'A lay sung in the temple of Minerva Girtonensis'.

> *Aemila Girtonensis*
> *By the Nine Muses swore*
> *That the great house of Girton*
> *Should suffer wrong no more*
> *By Muses Nine she swore it,*
> *And named a voting day*
> *And bade her learned ladies write*
> *And summon to the impending fight*
> *Their masters grave and gay.*
> *Shame on the Cambridge Senator*
> *Who dares to lag behind*
> *When female voices call him*
> *To improve the female mind.★*

The victory, however, was due to Pollia Nunamensis (could this be Mrs Henry Sidgwick?) who 'of Cupid's arrows seized a pair'.

★ Charles Whibley, *In Cap and Gown*, 1898, p. 326.

The higher education of women was still felt to be a single Cause, and this to be more than a local triumph.★ Miss Smith of Oxford, who had created a University College at Bedford by her bold forcing action as Reid Trustee, heard at once, and

> It is remembered by students of the time how on the 24th of February, 1881 – the day when Graces allowing women to take the Tripos examinations at Cambridge were passed – she burst into the dining room at Bedford College, where they sat at dinner, crying excitedly 'We have won! We have won!'†

★ *Life at Girton College,* by a Girton Student, was printed in 1882 as a modest advertisement; in the same year *The Girton Review* began, and has appeared continuously ever since.

† Margaret J. Tuke, *A History of Bedford College for Women,* 1939, p. 326.

Chapter 3

THE COLLEGE EVOLVES, 1881-1926

IN the years between 1881 and 1926, two phases of constitutional development succeed. The reign of Emily
Davies which lasted till 1904, was filled with a gigantic
building programme, for which she grabbed every penny
that came to the College, leaving Girton with several miles
of corridor, with spacious accommodation for 180 undergraduates – most of whom enjoyed not one but two rooms
of their own – and with a heavy load of debt. The second
phase (1904–26) saw an internal building programme of
equal importance. Physically, the place remained unchanged,
for what was there remained to be paid for; but self-government developed, advanced study and research began. This
new movement – largely due to the influence and shaping
policy of former students – also reflected the growing
power and independence of the teaching body, who
reached out beyond the college to link it with university
teaching and with the world outside. Thus Girton as an
institution matured of itself, anticipating moves towards
integration with the university; titular degrees were
awarded in 1921, the College Charter was granted
in 1924; women were admitted to university teaching office,
and to membership of the Faculties and Faculty Boards
in 1926.

Since there were but two, the Cambridge women's colleges grew on a scale which few women's colleges elsewhere
could achieve. The wise financial policy for Girton which
had been laid down by Mr Tomkinson was pursued by the

remarkable first resident Bursar, Eleanor Margaret Allen (1906–29); and a number of Cambridge men gave generously of their time by serving on the executive body. In this period, Girton was virtually refounded in the sense that it was brought close to the true collegiate form of government without any spectacular external change being apparent; this silent revolution, accomplished during the period up to and including the First World War, enabled the college to meet opportunities which fell to women in the early nineteen-twenties – if only after they had gained the franchise, entry to Parliament and to every other university in the British Isles.

Emily Davies had no ambition to hold the Mistress-ship – especially after the move to Cambridge. She herself was not a scholar, nor the member of a particularly scholarly family; she would not have felt at ease in a society to which the founders of Newnham naturally belonged. Her intellectual roots were in London, in the movements started by F. D. Maurice, in the 'Langham Place' group of feminists, and the schools commission. Although the College was her greatest achievement, it did not represent the sum total of her commitments. Rather, it stood as summit of an educational pyramid; and consequently she thought of it as a training place for teachers, with something of the structure of a school. During the period that followed her return to London, her shaping principles were: first, the absolute priority of rapid expansion to meet needs of 'the multitudes outside', and therefore the priority of building over advanced study or any rival claims to money; secondly, complete division between the executive power and the College teaching staff. If Girton did not become malformed in the same way as some of the earlier foundations, good fortune waited upon the tenacity of those who were prepared to

oppose Miss Davies; for her, the College for Women remained a national, not a local institution. Opposition was
not easy, for after her retirement from the mistress-ship in
1875, Miss Davies virtually ran the London Executive Committee. When she was not herself acting as secretary or
treasurer, she delegated to her relative, Mrs Croom Robin-
son; Mr Tomkinson's ill health obliged him to resign the
treasurership to Miss Davies in 1877. He thought that she
gave too little freedom of action to the Mistress and
told her it was 'wire pulling from a distance'. With Mme
Bodichon also incapacitated, Lady Stanley of Alderley alone
among the founders was able to exert a strong counter-
influence. The Committee often met at her London house
but it had no regular chairman; a name was proposed at each
meeting. However, from 1880 it included three members
nominated by the University of Cambridge.

Miss Davies felt that those concerned in running the
establishment should not also have power over its finances.
In spite of her insistence on independent lives for young
women, there was one kind of independence to which she
remained oblivious. It was ten years before the Mistress was
co-opted to the Executive Committee and even then not as a
full member. Miss Welsh, as a daughter of the College, was
in no position to oppose Miss Davies; a charming, vivacious
Irishwoman, who won the students' confidence and handled
them with tact, she cared for people rather than planning,
becoming the social head of the society till in later years she
overtaxed her strength. So in spite of growing restlessness
and growing organisation of Old Girtonians, firmly expressed at their annual meetings, the one influence predom-
inated. With the advent of the next Mistress, Miss Constance
Jones, in 1903, her position on the Committee became
established and Miss Davies gracefully withdrew. The focus

shifted rapidly from London to Cambridge, by orderly transfer of the executive.*

In 1910 the first Girton Fellowship for Research was established. The number of teaching officers had increased too; the shape of the Senior community was changing, though not as rapidly as the College's outward form.

Miss Davies's building policy and Miss Welsh's gifts as a landscape gardener meant that by the opening of the new century, the College was physically in being, almost in its present form. A vast edifice in three main courts – C. S. Lewis once termed it 'The Castle of Otranto' – its massive unity and solidarity spoke of the founders' tenacity of purpose, their belief in a grander future. The period piece has by now acquired a period charm, and some period discomforts. It was designed for a huge series of coal fires, maintained by a large number of servants – there used to be little sitting-rooms for the maids on the New Side and a series of bell-pulls in each gyp wing. It takes up an enormous acreage and is not at all easy to maintain; latterly the mere repairing of the chimneys – no longer used, they began to fall – swallowed up a sum equal to the first great benefaction. Very little of the old building has been left unmodified; yet wherever it is

---

* 1904 Miss Mary Clover (a young friend of Miss Davies) succeeded her as secretary, still living in London; but the Education Board was created in the College.

1906 Miss Allen became resident Bursar.

1908 The secretary removed to Cambridge and took up office in the College.

1909 A permanent Chairman was appointed and the Committee met in Cambridge.

1910 A staff representative was nominated to the Executive Committee.

1911 The Executive Committee was replaced by a College Council.

1911 The Old Girtonians' organisation reorganised as the College Roll.

necessary to make a change, the beautiful old workmanship reveals itself. No two rooms are made to exactly the same measurements, the sets of windows always have some difference, so that in spite of its great scale, there remains great diversity within the building; those who remember the little corners, the Gothic arches, the turret staircases, the queer little eccentricities of some especial corner will feel a special devotion that resists all change. Former students who return want first to see their own room.

The finest period piece is the Stanley Library – its companion pieces have been modernised. I remember in my undergraduate days one sunny afternoon climbing into a ground-floor room that was always kept locked. It was a small science Lab and stood at the end of Orchard Wing unused, though the larger one remained behind Old Wing as the last college Lab in Cambridge. In the dusty old room I found blue patterned Morris tiles in the sinks, Art Nouveau Bunsen burners and a large wooden case. Opening this, I was confronted by a completely articulated skeleton that had above it a little brass plate 'In loving memory of . . .' The skeleton remained till quite recently and, as a complete figure is something of a rarity, could often be seen lolling in the back of a car, waiting to be taken on a trip to Cambridge.

Just outside the door of this Bluebeard's chamber stood a bust of Mr Gladstone on a pedestal; it used to be alleged that one of the maids coming along that corridor in the gloom mistook it for a ghost and screamed aloud. Mr Gladstone was disposed of and his handsome pedestal sold to a monumental mason. The staircase below which he stood was also a haunted spot; here could be seen the 'Grey Lady' – the girl who had died before coming to college, and whose father had built the 'Taylor Knob' in her memory. By the eighties the College had its ghosts – including the ghosts of some extinct purposes, ruling from the past.

Lady Stanley gave the library in 1884, the Laboratory in 1877 and she also built a gate lodge. In the previous year the College had received its first great benefaction from a lady previously unknown to its members. In 1852 Jane Catherine Gamble, a wealthy spinster, was pursued to Italy by an adventurer named Henry Wikoff – not altogether without encouragement. He abducted her and held her in a palace at Genoa; but she kept him at bay, avoiding a fate worse than death, and Wikoff was sentenced to imprisonment for eighteen months.*

She left her fortune to a woman's college so that no man should benefit by it, together with a collection of books, several trunks of manuscript plays of her own composition, a marble statue of Lorenzo de Medici, and a portrait of herself with a romantic and melting expression, leaning upon a guitar.

Emily Davies, moving forward at once, started another building programme, in a style more opulent and less elegant than the Old Court; The building extended in Tower Wing, with heavily timbered gables, a tower that is Tudor at the base and Norman at the top, and that boasts at one side a little turret for the novelty of a telephone, at the other a Tricycle Room for convenience of visiting lecturers. The second Waterhouse built this piece of Scottish Baronial in flamboyant emulation of great College gatehouses.

When Miss Davies produced a yet larger scheme, however, the Executive Committee rebelled, and led by Lady Stanley of Alderley, staved off a further expansion for seven years. Mr Tomkinson, who now suffered severely from

* See Henry Wikoff, *My Courtship and its Consequences*, 1855, and Duncan Crow, *Henry Wikoff, The American Chevalier*, (London 1963).

ill-health, was unable to intervene, and after Lady Stanley's death Miss Davies succeeded in pushing through a programme which left the college in debt for the sum of £40,000.

Miss Davies's complete and utter concentration on building may have been due to long remembrance of that early failure, when she and Mme Bodichon set out to raise £30,000 and collected only £2,000. To the end, as far as she was able, she herself contributed generously, but Lady Stanley, a far larger benefactor, maintained her opposition. The buildings of 1897–1902 were on a truly grand scale; the new Hall measures only a few feet less than the hall of Trinity and can accommodate 280 at a meal. This effort served as a silent protest to Cambridge, which had once again refused to open degrees to women; what began as an anticipation of victory remained as a physical gesture of self-assertion and independence.

The last successful battle of Miss Davies concerned the building of the College Chapel. To this Lady Stanley had been opposed on grounds of belief as well as expediency. Later Victorian Cambridge had witnessed a severe struggle for freedom of religious belief. At Girton daily prayers had been said in what is now the linen room, and Sunday services conducted in the Old Hall after supper (where the smell of roast mutton effectually precluded the possibility of more conventional incense). Emily Davies was quite determined to have a chapel and was ready to start a private fund for it. On the plans it was cunningly described as 'the chapel or prayer room' and hints were thrown out that it might be used for lectures. When in May 1902, the building was completed, a double service was conducted by Miss Davies's brother and by the Rev. A. H. Cooke of King's who had long officiated at Sunday service, but there was no formal consecration. Miss Davies chose the motto carved over the doorway – *Hucusque auxiliatus est nobis Dominus* – Hitherto the Lord hath been our helper. This wholly Emilian and slightly admonitory use of the Book of Samuel reminded the Deity, so to speak, of His further responsibilities.

While building proceeded, the informal parts of the garden were laid out by the Mistress, who also had held the office of garden steward from 1883. Here, Miss Welsh was helped by the generosity of a London headmistress, Miss Fanny Metcalfe. Hawthorn and laburnum were set round the edge of what is now the lacrosse field, the yew hedge and the Honeysuckle Walk were planted, and Lady Stanley gave a rustic summer-house, which used to stand at the bottom of the Walk. The pond was dug, and a Japanese bridge built over it. When more land was purchased, a small golf course appeared for a decade, then vanished in 1901. More land was bought to the west, making over fifty acres. Then the full sweep of the Woodlands walk was designed by Miss Welsh from the top of the new Tower, and the beauty of her planting still remains – single trees on the lawns, glades and thickets beyond.

From the single silver birch that sweeps its long boughs across the sunset in the old court, the cedar outside the Stanley Library, to the close clump of limes in Woodlands Court that in autumn turns from gold to palest primrose and then to a delicate lattice of boughs against the East Anglian morning skies, to the massed glades of the park lands – prospect varies, wing by wing. Farther out in the garden come the tulip trees, the mulberry and judas, the metasequoia by the pond (of a later planting), the lilac bushes of dark purple and lavender, creamy white and pale blue; the thick lavender hedge at the Grange annexe that stands where the view is widest, west to Madingley hill and over a Dutch pastoral scene to Fenstanton. Chestnut trees with their spiky candles are set ranked in the drive; in little wild glades where whitethorn overhangs the bluebells and cowslips, a gold-finch or a woodpecker may be found, though nightingales come no longer.

No college in Oxford or Cambridge can boast such a setting, and as its beauty changes with the season, it feeds the beauty of the countryside into the mind, preserving some-thing of that privacy which Emily Davies intended, though she herself took no part in its creation.

Miss Davies continued to oppose any representation of the college lecturers or even the presence of the Mistress on the Executive Committee. In defeat she was, as ever, calm and unruffled; at the age of 72, she still had many years of life before her and, as long as she could, came to visit the College regularly and to take part in the gathering of old students. She lived to see the Jubilee celebrations of 1919, and to re-ceive messages from those assembled, though she was too enfeebled to attend. The Old Court was named after her in 1912, but her only public recognition was the honorary degree of LL.D from Glasgow University in 1910; she was among the first women to receive it.

A fully corporate college with its present and former students, its present and former fellows, takes something of the shape of a family; thus, one of the effects of consolidation was to substitute the impersonal family structure of the institution itself for an association based on actual dynastic succession. Miss Davies had been accustomed to work through 'those we know and can trust' – the first mistresses and officers of the committee had been from within her circle, and from this circle, very skilfully, she chose her own youthful successor. Madame Bodichon's cousin Barbara Shore Nightingale held a number of posts and became the college historian; Lady Stanley's daughter, the Countess of Carlisle, proved a most generous benefactor, and her granddaughter came to Girton as a student; Miss Jex Blake was succeeded in the mistress-ship by her cousin, Dame Bertha Phillpotts.

The ten years between Miss Davies's retirement and the outbreak of war were dominated by the enormous debt that building had imposed. It was cleared in 1914 by the advance of an unknown benefactor. Miss Clover used to describe how, in May 1913 when strenuous exertions had reduced the amount to £24,000, she received a letter stating that an anonymous person would pay £12,000 if an equal sum could be raised within that year. She gave the letter to her chairman, half afraid he might dismiss it as a hoax, which indeed it was by some believed to be; but the Council bravely ventured on a big campaign, and at the end of the year, by the most extraordinary efforts, had actually raised the sum required. The secretary then went to the solicitor to whom she had been directed, only to find that he knew nothing of the arrangement. However, she was given another address, to which she went anxiously, and such was her agitation that she drove round and round Piccadilly Circus in a hansom, long unable to find the place. At last, she deposited her note, and eventually the cheque arrived. It came from Sir Alfred Yarrow, the shipbuilder, a powerful and eccentric old man.*

So at the outbreak of war, the college stood clear of debt, even blessed with a small surplus. Miss Davies suggested that

* According to Miss Clover, he always slept most soundly when at sea, and therefore had a swinging cot built, which had a mechanism that suggested the rocking of a ship. This he took round with him to hotels and anywhere else he happened to be staying.

a new building fund should be started; but other courses prevailed and it was set aside for endowment.

From the time when Archdeacon Cunningham was appointed first permanent chairman of the Executive Committee in 1909, the growth of a collegiate structure began. He inaugurated a number of practical measures, long overdue. He was succeeded briefly by the Master of Caius, Sir Hugh Anderson, then by Arthur Berry of Trinity who had been on the Executive Committee for many years, and who, with Sedley Taylor and Henry Mather Jackson, might be said to have given the college its roots in the University; later, by the Master of Emmanuel, Peter Giles.

The First World War brought stresses and strains. Cambridge emptied of men, and the women's colleges found themselves working almost alone. Some members went off to the Balkans with the Scottish Women's Ambulance; Ethel Sargant began a National Register of professional women; the College Secretary became also the secretary of the First Eastern General Hospital, housed in huts on the future site of the University Library.

As a result of public need, in 1916 women were admitted to medical examinations, the first concession given since 1881. When in the year following the Armistice, Girton celebrated its Jubilee, many must have hoped that this heralded the full admission of women to the university. But the vote was lost; once again as in that other Jubilee time, 1897, London trains brought down the non-placets; the rhymesters brought out their ancient jibes, the gates of Newnham were stormed by a mob.

Self-government was enhanced when Miss Jex Blake succeeded to the mistress-ship (1916–22), finally to be shaped by her cousin and successor, Bertha Phillpotts (1922–25). Katharine Jex Blake who had resided in the College all her working life, knew all the students from the beginning except those very few who came up before 1879. A formidable and authoritative character, a superb teacher of the classics, with a biting wit and the confidence of a scholarly background – in her, for the first time, the College found a Mistress who both in character and attainments could make an impression commensurate with her full role.

This was the generation of the Strong-Minded Dons who gradually took over the lead from the Old Girtonians. M. B. Thomas, who taught science, refused to pay her rates because she did not have a parliamentary vote, and had sometimes to be rescued from the consequences of this stand. Eileen Power, who taught history from 1913 to 1921, was youthful enough to be close to the students, her wit lightened by beauty and gaiety. Bertha Phillpotts had served in the embassy at Stockholm during the war, and to great administrative gifts added a passion for research. When her cousin retired, and she succeeded to the mistress-ship, a Statutory Commission was sitting on the question of university administration. Bertha Phillpotts was the only woman member, and to her judgement and good sense the favourable outcome must be in some degree attributed. Under her guidance, the postgraduate studies which had been carried on by a few distinguished individuals were greatly expanded. Both Mistresses left on the college a stamp of excellence as scholars and administrators – they were the first of the moderns.

The First Girton Research Fellow, Mrs Arthur Strong, was elected for life in 1910; as a distinguished classical archaeologist she spent most of her working life in Rome, so that her influence in Cambridge was indirect. The first woman to take the Natural Sciences Tripos was a Hitchin student, Miss Kingsland; she briefly became a lecturer but when Lady Stanley gave the first laboratory in 1877, she was succeeded by Mrs Bidder, one of the first women to carry out independent work in Cambridge (1881–8), who taught at both Girton and Newnham. In true collegiate spirit, she cared for the little things as well as the great, and spent her leisure supplying students' rooms with bookshelves. As early as 1902 Mrs Hertha Ayrton (Sarah Marks) was proposed for the fellowship of the Royal Society. Ethel Sargant, who had started a laboratory in her mother's garden, was the first woman member of council of the Linnean Society; she came back to reside in Girton village in 1912.

In the early nineteen-twenties, horizons expanded. Some of the dons dressed beautifully (Elizabeth Drew went off to Paris to design dresses), they acquired sports cars, they went round the world, or handled small boats in high seas; some became rather less fixed to the College and inclined to go off in search of adventure elsewhere. The devoted tradition of Miss Cave and Miss Clover, Miss Allen and Miss Thomas was not for them, though none could be at once more devoted and more adventurous than P. K. Leveson, who wandered through the Far East after visiting her naval brother on the China Station, yet stayed in the service of the College till almost her eightieth year. Legends and sayings grew round these figures, the myths of an evolving college – such as the terrified freshman who apologised to Miss Jex Blake: 'Am I sitting on your chair?' to be answered, 'All the chairs are my chairs'; or the legendary domestic notices of P. K. adjuring students not to die in the gyp wings and to tie their bags firmly round the middle. These are schoolgirls' jokes, perhaps; and ties with certain schools became very strong. Some college rooms became traditionally associated with Cheltenham, St Paul's or Wycombe Abbey, and were handed down from student to student. Teaching remained the favoured profession of the College graduate, although a strong missionary tradition was also established. Partly because of its isolation, partly because of these traditions, and partly because of its record, the devotion of the Old Girtonians was of a deep and lasting kind. The College had depended on them for leading the movement towards self-government at a time when the senior resident members had little direct power; but the majority of these, of course, were also former students of the College. A similar development took place at Newnham, and at both colleges old students were given representation on the governing body.

The domestic staff also became part of the legend. Some have served the College for more than half a century – family groups of the Deans, Evans, Nightingales have provided their dynastic successions. Bertha Phillpotts introduced from Oxford the Portress Emily Hills, perhaps the most widely loved and known of all. On arrival, Emily did not unpack her trunks in the first week – but she stayed for over thirty years. Her tactful and discreet management of public relations sprang from a shrewd judgement which at the time of entrance examinations she would share with the dons. 'Oh, no, madam, I wouldn't have that one, she's a silly little thing . . . Now that other one, Oh, she *is* a nice young lady.' It was well to take note of Emily's verdict. She had a light, cool touch in any difficulty and shared many secrets.

As the new developments of the early twenties began, one more benefaction of the greatest importance came from Sir Alfred Yarrow, who in 1922 founded research fellowships in science with a capital sum of £40,000. This led to the election of a series of women whose distinguished contributions to science gave the College a fitting place in Cambridge among other centres of higher learning. The full story of their contribution is not within my powers; but the rapid progress of this work was one of its remarkable features, for Sir Alfred had stipulated that capital and income must be expended within twenty years. Fortunately, as his benefaction ran out, it was replaced by the bequest of Miss Edith Tucker, through which the work is now continued.

Miss Jex Blake had given a sum presented to her on retirement to endow a fellowship in arts; the Old Girtonians supported a research studentship; two more were endowed by Ottilie Hancock. In 1922 the university instituted the advanced degrees of Ph.D., M.Litt. and M.Sc., which women promptly entered for. (In the previous year it had again rejected the full admission of women.)

Finally the Charter (1924) gave almost complete self-government to the Mistress and those who now became Fellows of the College; although some representatives of the men's colleges and of the old students also remained on the governing body and the council. But any differences of form between the new College and the older Cambridge foundations were minimal and of a kind that its special circumstances required. After 1926 the distinctions between titular and full membership of the university became very slight. By admission of women to university lectureships the position of the teaching members had been made far more secure, and the College could afford to expand. It was still staffed like a school, that is, with Fellows appointed in all the main teaching subjects; though one or two scientists also gained permanent positions in virtue of research – Dr Ann Bishop F.R.S. was to remain continuously from 1922 as a member of the High Table, researching for the Medical Research Council.

Women were very generously admitted to teaching and examining and to membership of boards, the comparative centralisation of studies at Cambridge assisting here. When in the early nineteen-thirties I stayed at Somerville, I had already examined for Cambridge University, but found there ladies much senior to myself who had never so officiated. 'I prefer justice to favours,' one of them haughtily remarked to me, with a flash of old feminist spirit; but Cambridge felt it was more important to revise the Tripos syllabus than to protest at Q's habit of addressing his audience as 'Gentlemen'.

It was over thirty years after they had gained the right to national franchise that women were finally permitted to vote in the councils of the university. They had learnt what much longer lasting advantages sprang from moderation, conciliation and patience.

Chapter 4

WITHIN THE GATES 1926-1969

THOUGH growth and change slow down, a rising curve is traceable in the forty-odd years that have elapsed since women were admitted to titular degrees. Between 1926 and the end of the Second World War, an easy, regular advance was maintained within the stable society of the university; then after the war came the full admission of women (1948) into a society that was itself undergoing a very rapid change, as national and international educational policy played with increasing directness upon the university. A third college for women was founded; mixed institutions for graduates followed; the possibility of mixed under-graduate colleges has been established, though not put into practice. The traditional notion of a college is being chal-lenged. Looking back over these forty years, I seem to see a period of tranquillity, followed by one of disturbance and change, as yet unresolved.

In 1927 Girton had attained only about two-thirds of its present size; some dons still knew all the students, and main-tained a family atmosphere. On arrival we grouped into small parties, known as 'college families', who sat together in hall, sharing amusements, small tasks, special tastes and jokes. My 'family' consisted of four English students and three historians, but others were larger; members could drift away or join, yet the unity of the group was recognised by other groups. It held two schoolmates, otherwise it was a chance formation, which still, after forty years, retains some feeling of cohesion. Relations with the dons were distant, but once a week invited members put on full evening dress and dined at High Table. Behind the dining-hall, a small army hut served as private dining-room for the dons, where the Mistress would entertain groups of students informally.

Miss Major gave a pep talk to the freshmen which, though light and easy, ended with a recommendation to put on gloves and hats at Storey's Way, the half-way line to Cambridge – 'and remember, my dears, that the eyes of the Cambridge Ladies will be ever upon you'. Her Irish charm and genial worldly wisdom had conquered that little world, but she felt it was still to be approached cautiously. The chaperon rules which survived in vestigial form, were relaxed for those who had been to co-educational schools, and were unofficially ignored by many of the students. The Mistress was still directly responsible for all discipline – she was 'The Tutor', as in Miss Davies's day.

College societies still survived, but many did not really flourish; the fire brigade still rose to its early drills, and games were played vigorously. At a Freshers' Rag we engaged in decorous charades; at Christmas the party for gyps was preceded by a show of dolls, which they had dressed for the children at the University Settlement in Southwark. Carol singers went round the College at this time; at the end of the Lent Term, we all rose early to pick violets in the College garden; in the summer the freshers served early teas to those sitting the Tripos, and raised a faint feminine cheer as the College bus rumbled off from the College gate; on return there were Tripos teas in the Honeysuckle Walk. It was necessary to be in College by 11.15 each night, and buses were few. The College bus ran regularly however – as it does today; with the building of new colleges and development of new scientific departments in West Cambridge, the central focus of the university has shifted to bring Girton well within the orbit.

Quite a number of mixed clubs flourished – political and religious groups, C.U.M.S. and the Madrigals; in 1928, a Jesus man named Alistair Cooke founded the first mixed dramatic society, the Mummers. At Girton, the College play was given on a tiny stage erected in Hall, and with an all-feminine cast. Even for libraries, students relied on their own resources to a much greater extent than at present; the Bookworms' Society, which had once supplemented the College library, was however in decline.

In the thirties, distinction seemed to decrease with better lighting, more buses, and greater freedom of intercourse. The economic consequence of the slump and the political consequences of the rise of Fascism increased anxiety and led to students' communal action; Girton fed the hunger-marchers as they passed down the Huntingdon Road on their way to London. University prizes counted for much, and yet the young woman who chose advanced work might pass through very lean years, although the Women's Appointment Board was created at this time by the joint action of Girton and Newnham. One research fellow of Girton, quite without family resources, left to take a post as librarian at a resident salary of £100 a year. The first refugees began to arrive – in 1933 Lotte Leubuscher, first woman professor of Economics in the University of Berlin, finding herself ejected, came back to her English college. She used to return to visit her mother, braving the Nazi thugs who shadowed her on these trips. 'He climbed into the railway carriage, said "Heil Hitler", and sat down with his arms folded, his boots and revolver shining. I just folded my arms too and glared back at him.' She had a very straight blue glance. Julian Bell and John Cornford were killed in Spain; the ominous cloud

74

darkened. A schoolgirl refugee arrived from Czechoslovakia. Gas masks were issued from the village school.

Up to the mid-thirties there was a well-established social hierarchy at the High Table, some of whom had known Miss Davies's régime. In the mid-thirties a whole group retired together; younger and more rebellious dons came to the fore; married fellows appeared, and one used semi-surreptitiously to harbour husband and baby on the premises. The College Director of Studies no longer occupied an academic summit, since university posts were competitive; moreover with the start of a tutorial system, the responsibility for students was distributed.

Social inflexions had subtly changed; this, if one of personal stress, was yet a period of comparative opulence for the College as a whole. The new Fellows' Rooms, added in 1933, made entertainment on a proper scale possible for the first time. The New Wing gave modern standards of comfort – at least for the few. The Library, by a generous benefaction from Thomas McMorran, was splendidly rehoused. The garden became one of the great sights of Cambridge in summer time, Miss Butler's garden by the pond vying with the rockery at the Grange.

The war years involved contraction of activities but in other ways Girton escaped lightly. In early days, evacuees from Queen Mary College shared the buildings, till they found premises of their own; the garden was turned over to pigs and vegetables; the Grange annexe was occupied by the army.

However, only three fellows left the college for full-time war service, though the remainder bore a heavy burden of teaching, often doing duty for men who were away. Undergraduate courses were slightly curtailed, but far more academic activity continued than during the First World War.

In 1945, the transition was smoothly made. A few ex-service women came as students by way of a special examination, but general changes developed only gradually. As before, they followed larger changes in society as a whole, and though some legal modifications were made, the more important and less explicit consequences revealed themselves gradually.

In 1948, the admission of women to full membership of the university threw open the last gates – those of university administration. The central committees which directed policy, such as the General Board of the Faculties, the Council of the Senate and the Financial Board could accept women at the very moment when the practice of self-government had developed one or two excellent administrators. Admission to syndicates and to these central committees was more than a matter of gratification to those concerned and to their colleagues; it became immensely valuable as, under the pressure of national policy, the university grew increasingly centralised. In 1945, Girton was run as a small free self-regulating economic unit. Since that date, fees have had to be brought in line with those charged elsewhere, policy of employment scales and of the privileges that go with them has been shaped to the model of the university. A university contribution is paid by the college. Its accounts are drawn in the approved fashion for Cambridge colleges. Its freedom of manœuvre has thus been much restricted, but the advantage of becoming part of a larger system acts as compensation. Owing to the rapid growth of scientific departments, as well as general educational trends, higher education soon became a national responsibility and in spite of their separate identities and tradition of autonomy, this reacted powerfully on all colleges.

Membership of the university brought in salaries which

very largely paid for college teachers, and enabled a rapid expansion of the fellowship; at present it is fifty five. This met and matched an expansion in the student membership. After the war, when the small number of places available at Cambridge for women became the subject of general concern, Girton rapidly enlarged her numbers to the limit allowed for women, three hundred students, by cutting up the old double sets, and giving each student a bed-sitting-room. Some of the old-style sets remained – where construction made such division impracticable – but in effect, with no increase in overhead administration, comparatively small expenditure, and some discomfort Girton augmented its membership by a number almost equalling that of a new foundation. So quietly was it done, that this contribution to women's education passed almost entirely unrecognised. Newnham also increased its numbers and purchased houses in the vicinity of the college, allowing other students to reside in approved lodgings.

Meanwhile the movement for establishing a third college was growing. New Hall opened in 1954, with two senior members, both of whom were former members of the Girton High Table – Miss Rosemary Murray, a Tutor and Lecturer teaching chemistry, and Miss Robin Hammond, a former lecturer in English.

The shape of the university was itself changing under the growth of new scientific departments, with emphasis on research. (Since 1939 the number of research students has increased in the university from about 350 to 2,000, whereas undergraduates have increased only from about 6,000 to about 9,000). A rising number of overseas members was promoted by new international grants. Thus, while the university became financially geared to national educational policy (which financed new departments and appointments through industry and the University Grants Committee) it was socially becoming a more international centre. A considerable quantity of fringe institutions collected, from schools of modern languages and coaching establishments to research centres. The social unit was no longer as homogeneous as it had been. In such a situation, lack of full membership would have been far more disabling than at an earlier time.

To mark the full admission of women to Cambridge, an honorary degree was accepted by the Queen, now Queen Elizabeth the Queen Mother, who also became Visitor of Girton College – a medieval office created by the Charter. Her Majesty visited the college, greeted by students who were wearing full academic dress, by the fellows, the college servants, and the scholars of Girton Village School, assembled in the drive and enthusiastically waving Union Jacks. Her Majesty stopped in the court to admire the gardener's baby, held in the arms of its mother, and to extend a finger, which the baby grabbed. 'How old is your baby?' she asked, and the gardener's wife, overcome by this attention, replied 'Six months, your Majesty', although her child was really nine months old. 'Dear me' said the Queen, benevolent but ever so slightly astonished, 'it's a *very* fine child.'

Nineteen fifty-two brought a second Charter giving the College the same form of government as the men's colleges, and leaving the Mistress and Fellows in full, unshared control. It was most fortunate that, as administrative burdens increased, a superb and tested team had evolved, which enabled this situation to be met because the regular procedure was running so smoothly. As numbers for the entrance examination rose, no one but K. M. Peace could have coped with the situation and combined it with the duties of College Secretary, as third in line from Miss Davies. The Bursar, the Registrar of the Roll, and the Mistress herself were all carry-

The First Degree. October 21st 1948. Her Majesty the Queen (Queen Elizabeth the Queen Mother, Visitor of Girton College) receives the Honorary Degree of LL.D.

ing double burdens, yet Girton in the fifties was better
organised than ever before, and only towards the end of this
period, with the retirement of some members did it become
essential to codify procedures, and set them down, formally,
for posterity.

Within the College framework administration inevitably
grew in scope. Tutors' duties doubled and trebled in these
years. At the same time, half the fellowship – more than half,
nearly three-quarters – were married women, chiefly those
'Cambridge Ladies' who had formerly been objects of
anxious concern. Here a new problem arose. The absence
of domestic help, joined with family responsibilities, imposed
great strain on these women, especially when they felt the
need also to play a part in university teaching and to pursue
independent work of their own.

'You can do three things,' one elderly sage told a young
college fellow, 'but you can't do four things at once'. So that
some elected to cut out all forms of administration, while
raising a family, teaching and writing books; others were
content sharply to limit their domestic responsibilities (and
here the heroic role of the Cambridge husband must be recorded), while yet again one or two contracted out of university teaching. The pattern of the married woman teacher or
administrator is varied, and it is necessary for the college to
appreciate this, and to adopt flexible forms which will take
advantage of whatever amount of work can be offered. For
by uniting the Cambridge world in new ties, such women
have something to offer their undergraduates and the community that is exceedingly precious. In recognising them,
Girton again played a pioneering part.

At the same time, the problem of Senior residence became
even more acute for the women's colleges than for the men's.
A small number of resident fellows is essential for order and

a collegiate social life; yet it is even more difficult for the young married woman than for the young married man to spare much time for college entertainment and residence.

Notwithstanding, the College retained much of its old special qualities. When in 1947 the Commemoration Fund was launched to celebrate the admission of women to the university, former students responded with the greatest generosity. Those who could, gave their thousands; those who were poor, sold their jewellery, or their old college gowns. In all £40,000 was collected. Subsequently, Miss Major left her estate to the college; the son of Sarah Woodhead, one of the three 'Pioneers', left a large sum; a research scholarship was founded by one old student; Mme Bodichon's library was presented by another. Old traditions did not disappear; they were perhaps most passionately affirmed by those who were most keenly aware of new developments.

For instance, Jean Lindsay founded what is now the Graduates' Union Society to deal with the problem of the lonely and unattached graduate student; but she dealt with this problem through the old ways of college hospitality which she had from her don M. G. Jones. The society is now institutionalised, thanks largely to the further efforts of a Newnhamite, Greta Burkill. In this practical work women gave a decisive lead. The Women Graduates' Club, founded after the war, has now merged in a much larger university institution, which has succeeded to its premises as well as its traditions. The Women's Research Club, founded in the early nineteen-twenties by another Newnhamite, survives in spite of the growing fragmentation of learning, and helps to hold together younger and older women, those who are fellows of colleges and those who are attached to other institutions.

It was not till the sixties that social changes in the relation of the university and colleges began to take structural form.

Nearly all tensions may be traced to the rapid increase of numbers, the much less homogeneous nature of Faculties, and economic stress; all of these weakened the position of the colleges. In 1864 Leslie Stephen could look forward with a prophetic eye to the arrival of women undergraduates 'looming in the distance of futurity' and to married Fellows, but he did not imagine the advent of professorial rule.

> Our plan is not to teach anyone anything, but to offer heavy prizes for competition in certain well-defined intellectual contests. . . . As most of the professors lecture upon topics which have no particular bearing upon these contests, upon Sanscrit perhaps, or Archaeology or History or Political Economy, or some equally useless and absurd subject, few people go to hear them.
>
> I will only add that our professors are ill paid, because the university as distinct from the colleges is very poor . . .*

It is now the colleges who are poor; professors who are the heads of large departments may wield more power than the head of a college. The heavy prizes now barely cover the cost of typing a prize essay, and have been replaced by grants from Government and from learned foundations or from industry. All but two or three of the colleges are to some degree dependent upon central funds, which come to them either in salary for their Fellows, or in the form of students' fees.

The general social problems facing a college today are discussed in Chapter 6. The older family atmosphere of colleges no longer reflects general social conditions since family ties in general have weakened, and both home and overseas students come from widely different ranges of society. Victorian Cambridge was closely related to the great public

* *Sketches from Cambridge*, pp. 89-91.

schools; the Cambridge of today is filled with those who are
seeking narrowly defined goals – this diploma, that qualification – and whose way has been opened by a series of public
grants. An undergraduate may feel himself to be one of an
intellectual *élite*, but he knows also that his school contem-
poraries may already be earning considerable salaries, marrying and buying a house, and the frustrating sense of being at
once privileged and restricted makes for anxious insistence
upon maturity.

Much is said about the forms of anxiety among students –
the incidence of nervous disturbance and of suicide. Or that
special form of moral suicide, drug addiction.

It is my impression that suicide is a good deal rarer among
women students than among men. In all my years at Girton
I can remember only three cases of suicide, as compared with
scores of young women who have been helped through their
difficulties to some form of adjustment.

For a young woman, the problems of her personal life
may induce much greater anxiety and become more dis-
ruptive in their consequences than those of the men. Family
stresses of a broken home leave heavy marks upon a young
woman; the personal decisions she makes on love and marriage may alter more drastically the possibility of study.
There have been cases of ill-assorted undergraduate marriages
that lasted only a few months, leaving the wife anxious to
return to study – but this is not always easy. There have been
other cases where marriage has given a deep reassurance that
was immediately reflected in intellectual freedom to concentrate and find self-expression.

I have seen some universities where students lived in
groups of commercial apartments, and ordered their own
life. On one far distant campus, where this district was
dubbed 'Sin City', the abortion rate was given me as 16

per cent of the annual feminine enrolment. Apart from its physical consequences, such an experience must be deeply disturbing to any woman of feeling; and psychologically ineradicable.

A small resident community of women may prove of particular value for the student from overseas who is coming to a different type of society from that which she has known. Many students from the Middle East or the emergent countries are facing the social problems that Englishwomen met a hundred years ago, when their own higher education was just beginning – the same prejudice, the same isolation. For such pioneers, a women's college provides a refuge, and to their parents and families perhaps offers a deeper reassurance. Girton has admitted a number of young Africans who have achieved impressive results.

With the university, the College has also become an international community; this benefits the young Englishwoman who, at an impressionable age, learns to live with those from very different regions. It is part of the duty of a college to see that this interchange continues.*

When Emily Davies planned her foundation, many women including married women, suffered from enforced idleness, and the frustration of Suburbia had already appeared.

It is objected that young women will only want a low place in the professional ranks because marriage will be their first duty. . . . It seems to be forgotten that women have always been married. Marriage is not a modern discovery, offering a hitherto untrodden field of action for feminine energy. The novelty is that, as has been said, the old field has been invaded and taken possession of by machinery. The married ladies of

* In 1948 Girton provided Harvard with the first woman to hold a university chair in that University, Helen Cam.

former days, instead of sitting in drawing-rooms, eating the bread of idleness, got through a vast amount of household business, which their successors cannot possibly do, simply because it is not there to be done.*

All the familiar modern argument about the domestic duties of motherhood are dealt with; but within a very different domestic setting. The married woman may now be aided by domestic appliances of a kind Emily Davies never envisaged, but she has lost the human support that once was taken for granted. The duties of a mistress in the household (remarked Miss Davies) are those of government and administration – managing the servants. At the beginning of this century domestic servants still formed the largest class of employed persons, with about four million women concerned – beside the voluntary service of maiden aunts, daughters of the family, and other unpaid assistants.

Today with a mere hundred and twenty thousand servants of both sexes, numbers are still declining. The modern educated woman will expect to have sole charge of a household. She will also expect to marry much earlier than was common a generation ago; in many cases directly upon graduation, or earlier. It is not easy to convince such young women that if they are to avoid boredom and frustration at a later stage, it is almost obligatory on them to undertake some form of work for a short period, even if this is not continued. The married woman whose children have grown to a point where they no longer occupy most of her time can regain employment if she has experience and training; but a degree, particularly an arts degree, does not in itself provide a competitive qualification. This investment in a future is of the greatest importance.

* *The Higher Education of Women*, Chapter 6.

The number of women undergraduates at Cambridge is under 900, as against some 1,400 at Oxford, or about one tenth of the total undergraduate population. Although in certain subjects popular with men, few women apply – such are law and engineering – yet problems of admission remain; mixed schools know it is easier to place boys, and the need for more women at Cambridge is nationally recognised. Girton College plans an expansion of numbers to mark the centenary. A new central site, to take carefully phased admissions, will in effect replace a projected fourth college for women by an experimental type of community, where the quickly changing patterns of student living may modulate. A 'dialogue' between the one centre and the other, and between our own college and others is hoped; the new project is conceived on the same national scale as was the original foundation and will make Girton eventually the largest women's college in Oxford or Cambridge.

Nevertheless, personal selection and personal commitment to the choice of a college by the student, with a choice of pupil by the teacher, remains the basis of college unity. Nothing is more fascinating than to find how knowledge of an individual grows in the process of admission. First there are the series of forms, from which a few facts are gleaned, perhaps the impression of a handwriting; then letters of recommendation; next the written papers, and finally the interviews. The outlines become clearer at each stage, the personality more definite, till finally a complete person emerges. This element of choice and commitment provides a true working relationship; and in many of the men's colleges, the women's system of admission is being approached.

When she arrives, the student in turn has to make a personal choice, not only between work and the dozens of social activities that Cambridge has to offer, but to evolve a style of life where all kinds of experiments in dress, behaviour, belief are practised. There are arts students who evolve a career in public relations, to which their academic work is subordinated. They are concerned to become actors, journalists, jazz musicians, or writers; they set about this in a professional way. Acting and to some extent journalism are easy for women to enter, but few of them give such wholehearted attention to this side of Cambridge life as the male undergraduate. Links with London are now well established in the professions, in the sphere of journalism particularly, where students may get retaining fees from London papers; for the university is 'news' and there is a tendency for life to copy the required image.

It would seem therefore that there is no lack of problems before Girton as it enters on its second century of existence, which ensures that a continuous process of refounding will proceed. The community may well become differently framed, since it is the social adjustment of the intellectual woman to the modern larger community that is the current problem requiring solution, and not, as a hundred years ago, the right to an intellectual life. But direct study of the re-integration of married women into working life (such as that undertaken at Radcliffe College, U.S.A.), and provision, perhaps, for the married undergraduate in greater numbers, must be related to the standards to be maintained at Cambridge – those standards which were so firmly adhered to by the founders. 'It won't do to blow the trumpet with an uncertain sound,' as Emily Davies declared.

Meanwhile, the mutual relations of colleges may grow closer, and perhaps a 'cluster' system may enable them at once to retain their identity and to pool their resources. It must not be assumed that changes in the school system will be without repercussions on the universities, or that the conflicts and stresses which have produced some new types of collegiate society have not already reshaped the traditional colleges. There is an open prospect.

But there is also an established identity. Both by its history and by the public idea of a women's college, Girton is committed in many ways. The roots are deep. The College for Women was founded upon an idea, and not merely to meet a temporary need. Perhaps for this reason, perhaps because of its historic precedence, Girton has symbolised the intellectual woman's life in popular literature; and though with her admission to full membership of Cambridge this symbolism is no longer so distinct, yet its traces remain as part of the living past within the present.

The very fact that the 'Girton Girl' is so unfashionable a figure in present-day terms may offer some protection and counterpoise to that vulnerable and sensitive little company who each year come up for the first time, and hear the modern version of that ironical wisdom that Miss Major proffered, forty years ago, to me.

Remember, my dears, the eyes of the Daily Screech will be ever upon you.

Part 2

THE SOCIAL IMAGE

Chapter 5

THE GIRTON GIRL: SOCIAL IMAGES FROM WITHIN AND WITHOUT

IN 1611 Ben Jonson described a society of Collegiate Ladies, though their study was scandal, and their campus the fashionable world. Neither the learned ladies of the Renaissance nor the Blue Stockings of the Augustan Age were given to association – they shone as single stars. Dr Johnson compared female preaching to a dog walking on its hind legs – 'it is not well done, but you are surprised to find it done at all'.*

As the first College for Women, Girton provided the focus for many fancies and dreams, and the 'Girton Girl' acquired a public identity which lasted into the present century. Legends that friends or enemies of women's education found congenial became attached to her. Works which had no connexion with education were sold under this interesting title; Miss Annie Edmonds in 1885 published a three volume novel entitled *A Girton Girl* where the heroine never even set her foot inside the College gates, because at the entrance examinations she met her handsome 'Fate'.

The History of Girton's literary reputation may be taken as an extended part of the College history, which still continues; for such a popular image, depicting the social assumptions made about women's education, and the fictional versions deriving from this image, may shape the institution itself, occasionally to acquiescence or, more commonly, to iconoclasm.

* Boswell, *Life of Johnson*. Entry for 31 July 1763.

Whether exploiting the novelty of a special environment, or written in protest, such works were almost certain if by women writers, to embody an ideal; if by men, to offer a mixture of gallantry and ridicule. The fear of women's achievements was shown indirectly, by making her either a competent imitator in manly occupations, or an absurd mimic of manly sports and the more crusty forms of academic ceremony (both being performed in feminine style).

Popular historians of Cambridge still betray a time-lag where the women's colleges are concerned. In 1940 the work of John Steegman based, as far as I am aware, on the very slightest acquaintance with women's colleges, retained the antagonism which denied entrance to women; while a more recent study by two fellows of King's College observes, 'One may not approve of girls being put under the exclusive supervision of middle-aged spinsters.'★ Both gentlemen are sons of women educated at Cambridge and must be perpetuating the stories they learnt at their mothers' knees. A glance at the residence list would have told them that about two-thirds of the women teaching at Girton are married, and further inquiry might have revealed that the majority are in their twenties or thirties.

The social history of all colleges is generally based on an obsolete conception, but this is more especially so with regard to the women's colleges; although at present the older universities enjoy a quite exaggerated news value, so that any story about them gains a ready press, often slanted to suit an outmoded 'image'.

In tracing the history of popular distortions, first the Cam-

★ Jasper Rose and John Ziman, *Camford Observed*, 1964, p. 165. John Steegman, *Cambridge*, published 1940; see especially pp. 41–2.

The most recent study of 'Cambridge and Society in Victorian England' Sheldon Rothblatt's *The Revolution of the Dons*, 1968, except for one inaccurate statement, ignores the foundation of the women's colleges.

bridge social versions and then the more extreme fictional versions of the nineteenth century will lead on to those fictional studies from within the walls, which have appeared since 1900.

Tennyson's poem, *The Princess*, was written in 1847; it may have been inspired by his Cambridge friend, Frederick Denison Maurice, founder of Queen's College, Harley Street, and a prominent member of that Cambridge society, the 'Apostles', which exerted such a strong influence on the poet and his whole generation. Frederick Denison Maurice, a close friend of Emily Davies and of her brother Llewelyn, was concerned not only with women's education, but that of other deprived groups; so the story of Tennyson's *Princess* is framed in a picnic scene of a Mechanics' Institute, who are holding their summer fête in the grounds of a lordly estate, and demonstrating scientific joys by a mimic telegraph and galvanic shocks.

This fairy-tale 'medley' or dream of a women's college, an uneasy mixture of idyll and farce, reflects Tennyson's mixed feelings for women. 'He entertains at one and the same moment a feeling of almost adoration for them and an ineffable contempt', wrote Jane Welsh Carlyle – 'adoration, I suppose, for what they might be – contempt for what they are.'

On the gate of the College founded by Princess Ida is inscribed 'Let no man enter in on pain of death'; the princess, 'as grand as doomsday and as grave', is much given to exhortation:

> *O lift your nature up,*
> *Embrace our aims; work out your freedom. Girls,*
> *Knowledge is now no more a fountain sealed.*

The unsealing process, however, did not yet extend to that particular fount which Elizabeth Garrett and Emily Davies as her friend and counsellor were to open some twenty years later. A princely intruder – in feminine disguise – is discussing his future syllabus with the Principal:

> *'And yet,' I said,*
> *'Methinks I have not found among them all*
> *The anatomic.' 'Nay, we thought of that'*
> *She answer'd, 'but it pleas'd us not; in truth*
> *We shudder but to dream our maids should ape*
> *Those monstrous males that carve the living hound,*
> *And cram him with the fragments of the grave,*
> *Or in the dark dissolving human heart*
> *And holy secrets of the microcosm,*
> *Dabbling a shameless hand with shameful jest,*
> *Incarnalise their spirits.'*

No wonder Miss Davies alluded to the work with displeasure; not only did it introduce that 'serpent', a separate institution for women, but also a separate course of study; such a work, however ardent in places could not but embarrass those who wanted to bring down the New Jerusalem to Hitchin Hill. The 'medley', as it was termed, presented lady proctors crying 'Name!' and eight strong daughters of the plough – the proctors' 'Men' – thrusting out any intruders. Women's aspirations are applauded only in order to be mocked. The discovery that three of her recruits were men in disguise caused the Princess in rage to miss her footing on a bridge, plunging headlong, so to speak, into the Cam. Rescued thence by her offending undergraduate lover, she capitulates, and the Ladies' College is voluntarily dissolved, with a perfect invocation of Trinity Great Court in a midsummer's night, and a Batchelors' Ball in progress.

THE GIRTON GIRL: SOCIAL IMAGES

Now sleeps the crimson petal, now the white,
Now waves the cypress in the palace walk;
Now winks the goldfin in the porphyry font,
The firefly wakens; waken thou with me . . . .

In the Lent Term of 1891, *The Princess* was given at
Girton by third year students – to an audience of Girtonians
and Newnhamites. By this time, it in turn had been gently
mocked in opera by Messrs Gilbert and Sullivan, and was
sufficiently removed from the established truth to be treated
with levity.

From the first, the womanly charms of young academic
aspirants had appealed to *Punch*, where a character named
Miss Hypatia Jones appeared. Notices of events treated the
young ladies of Hitchin to a little agreeable rallying.

THE CHIGNON AT CAMBRIDGE
At the examination lately held at Cambridge, a number of
students from the Ladies' College at Hitchin passed their Little-
Go; the first time that such undergraduates ever underwent that
ordeal. It is gratifying to be able to add, that of all those flowers
of loveliness, not one was plucked. (*14 January, 1871*)

Nine years later, *Punch* accepted the mathematical triumph
of Charlotte Angas Scott as a pleasant surprise, in contrast
with the shocking efforts of the 'Lancashire Witches' who
were still worshipping the idol of Women's Suffrage (7
February, 1880). The strategy of Miss Davies in temporarily
renouncing her political interests was justified in its effect on
public opinion.

In 1879, the American wife of R. C. Jebb described the
advantages of Girton and Newnham to some young rela-
tives; young women 'as a reaction from husband-hunting,
are throwing themselves into all sorts of things that promise

95

interest or a career'. She also mentioned, however, that a young American heiress has come to Girton, who keeps a pair of horses and a manservant, and who 'will, I have no doubt, with her fortune and position, marry here!'*

When Agnata Frances Ramsay was placed alone in the First Division of the First Class for the Classical Tripos of 1887, *Punch* saluted her with the cartoon 'For Ladies Only', and the Queen herself sent Miss Ramsay a signed photograph in token of approval. Almost immediately, like Tennyson's Princess, she succumbed to the wooing of the Master of Trinity, thus becoming the First Lady of Cambridge society. 'It is her goodness, not her Greek and Latin, that have stolen my heart', said the bridegroom; but the strengthening influence of Mrs Butler as a member of one of the great Cambridge families can be seen today in the achievements of her sons.

Another great Cambridge family partnership founded Newnham. When as a young bachelor of 33, Henry Sidgwick gave up his long vacation and summer holiday to start a residence for ladies, he felt 'I am going to have all the fun of being married without the burden of a wife'†, but in due time he married Eleanor Balfour; and as they took up their residence in Newnham, where she was Vice-principal and Bursar, they provided a model domestic arrangement which allowed this gentleman to become in many ways the representative of women's interests in the later years of the nineteenth century. Sidgwick, who after an undeserved setback was elected Professor of Moral Philosophy, brilliant and multifarious in activities, and Mrs Sidgwick, with the makings of a Wrangler, so efficient yet so unobtrusive and gentle, together were largely responsible for the graces of 1881 which

* M. R. Bobbitt, *With Dearest Love to All,* p. 149.
† *Henry Sidgwick, A Memoir,* p. 247.

HONOUR TO AGNATA FRANCES RAMSAY!
(CAMBRIDGE, JUNE, 1887.)

admitted women to examination; he also led the next move for the full admission of women. In the year of Queen Victoria's Diamond Jubilee this came to the vote and split Cambridge; the battle this time raged between a conservative majority and a substantial minority of the university's own members. As a visitor saw it:

> *Of late they seemed not as before,*
> *   The peace of other days was dead;*
> *With difficulty they forebore*
> *   To hit each other on the head.*

As inescapable consequences of the new movement, the opposition forecast the demise of ultimate masculine prerogative, such as has not even yet occurred – Women Vice-Chancellors and Queen-Proctors ('and such a thing would not be nice'). Indestructible as the hydra, the 'serpent' feared by Emily Davies also once more reared his head.

> *Others held that women's ways*
> *   Destroyed our academic tone:*
> *The sisterhood should really raise*
> *   A seat of learning all their own.*

> *'Twixt Cam and Isis, where the two*
> *   Sets of professors might alight,*
> *A very perfect spot they knew,*
> *   And Bletchley Junction was the site.★*

Bletchley – just as far removed as Hitchin, but even safer since British Railways eventually cut it off – would have given territorial isolation combined with preceptorial dependence – a kind of Ladies' Annexe to both the academic clubs.

When this matter was put to a vote of the Senate, the scene resembled an election riot. Special trains ran from London, and the undergraduates were whipped up to a display of feeling that a first year Girtonian described with astonishment.

★ Owen Seaman, 'Quis pro Domina?' from *Horace at Cambridge*, p. 95.

Miss Welsh put up a notice that we were not to go into Cambridge without permission. The undergraduates were entirely off their heads. They met the special trains of M.A.'s and hired all the cabs in Cambridge for the Non Placets . . . they had two effigies, one with big feet for Girtonians and one with red hair as a Newnhamite. There were placards posted up, 'England expects every M.A. (N) to do his duty'. 'Get thee to Girton, Beatrice, get thee to Newnham, this is no place for you maids'. 'No woman shall come within a mile of my courts' . . . they went about with 'No Women' on their hats. The M.A.'s were waiting for the results on the grass outside the Senate House, under a shower of confetti, bombs, squibs and crackers . . . Outside Caius was a board with five huge hats, 'Arriet hats, labelled 'lecture hats' and as soon as the results were published these were thrown down and trampled underfoot. Windows were broken with rotten eggs and oranges . . . In the evening one effigy was put on a bicycle and that on top of a hansom cab and taken to Newnham. But Newnham had warning and the gates were locked. Professor Sidgwick said very quietly, 'Gentlemen, I think you had better go home' and they went . . .

. But at night . . . they pulled down all the theatre hoardings, the public notices on Parker's Piece, 80 yards of palings from the New Museums, which they carried intact into the Market Place, and all the wood they could get, including some of the railings of Queens' and made a huge bonfire. The police could do nothing . . . About midnight or later the Fire Brigade was turned out and put out the fire and dispersed them with the hose.*

The substance had been granted when women were admitted to examination, as Sidgwick had pleaded. What

* Letter of 24 June 1897, reprinted in the *Girton Review*, Michaelmas Term 1951.

was asked for was the symbol, the official status; it was the symbol that was defended with such passionate prejudice. A. J. Godley, who celebrated the event in 'The 1713 against Newnham' – this being the number of adverse votes – accused women of tyranny; Apollo speaks:

> *Rash youth! forbear ungallantly to vex*
> *Your fellow students of the softer sex!*
> *Ladies! proud leaders of our culture's van,*
> *Crush not too cruelly the reptile Man!*
> *Or by experience, you, as now, will learn,*
> *The eternal maxim's truth, that e'en a worm will turn.*†

But the ladies did not retaliate by adopting the methods of Mrs Pankhurst on the national issue. No one chained herself to the railings. Defenders of the *status quo* retained their monopoly of aggression, adding insult to injury by the imagined bathos of highly feminine protest:

Hemich a: *Horrid things! I really wonder any ever dared to come*
When they know to base Non Placets that we're always not at home.
Bemich: *'Tis a national dishonour; 'tis the century's disgrace!*
Hemich a: *If the college rules allowed it, I would like to scratch their face!*

Twenty-three years later, after a world war, in 1920, a petition for full membership was again rejected, the 'Serpent' again reared its head, the special trains ran once more, and once again the undergraduates mobbed Newnham, leaving Cambridge as the last university in England to deny to women the full degree.

† Jean Lindsay, *A Cambridge Scrapbook*, p. 114.

The College Fire Brigade, 1887

Students at work in the college laboratory

THE GIRTON GIRL: SOCIAL IMAGES

Through the eighties and nineties, however, excluded women drew closer together; Girton was in touch with women's colleges in Oxford and America; the *Girton Review* of the eighties carried letters from Vassar, Bryn Mawr and Smith Colleges. It was no longer thought quite so odd or dangerous to go to college. Academically more experienced, but provoked by an article in the *Fortnightly Review* from the pen of a lady novelist, attacking higher education, Girtonians began to think about further economic and social aims and to exhort each other; 'we should not allow our thoughts to run in such a narrow groove, and cut ourselves off so completely from the interests of the world without our college walls'. Should they try to found a working girls' club in London? Agnata Ramsay became the secretary, and it was done. The Women's University Settlement in Nelson Square, Southwark, opened within a year. 'It may be regarded as a colony of educated women among the un-educated who, however, were there to learn as well as to teach.' Accusations of 'presumption' were indignantly rebutted:

> We confer on them, but also, principally, on ourselves, the inestimable boon of learning to realise the strength and depth of the common brotherhood which outlives not only the ex-pediency of social life, but also the personal likings and affec-tions that so powerfully influence our lives.*

The problem of employment was scrutinised. 'The teach-ing profession to which most of us look naturally, is becom-ing every year overstocked,' and though Cambridge women 'may hope through the benefit we have enjoyed at college to find employment where others fail' employers received fifty or sixty applications for every vacancy. The Association

* *Girton Review*, July 1887.

of Assistant Mistresses had investigated journalism, poultry farming, wood engraving, dressmaking and cookery schools. Why not a profit-sharing firm of lady dressmakers? The future of office work, as expanded by telephone and type-writer, remained unguessed. Undergraduates explored; but progress and innovation belonged to their careers beyond the Cam, not beside it.

The spirit of Barbara Bodichon had prevailed, with her eager exploration of the world, her practical sense of social duty. The later careers of these young women showed a great range of solid down-to-earth engagement with the social problems of big cities. The founding of Hillcroft, a working women's college, the care of deprived children, an extended series of practical achievements absorbed the more adventurous; while perhaps as many as half the Girtonians went to teach in the girls' schools which were growing up all over the country as the schoolmistress replaced the governess, or in mission schools abroad.

For Emily Davies, no doubt, her college represented the top of the educational hierarchy; from her point of view the national structure had been completed and beyond the B.A. there was nothing except the M.A. So she positively refused an offer of research scholarships from a well-wisher at Caius, she regarded even a fourth year as a waste of time, which filled up a place in her Temple of the Muses at someone else's expense.

Meanwhile the students

> *Studied and played well*
> *As everybody knows*

- perhaps with irrational hope that if they played hockey and golf they would be judged near enough to the masculine to obtain 'the B.' and 'the A.' College songs became based on examinations and sport. Miss Ramsay's triumph evoked new songs demanding recognition from 'the Lords of the Camus.'

> *For Girton has shown us again and again*
> *That the women can equal, nay, distance the men,*

but the little community became locally even more self-contained; the students, now much younger, arrived in their late teens, and by a much smoother route. They were neither as exceptional as the Pioneers nor as much an object of curiosity. This has been termed 'the High School period', during which the enforced parochialism was accepted without much attempt at alteration.

Physically the college grew at great speed as Emily Davies and the London Committee put every penny into building, but the spirit of the founders could not be so easily handed on. The biting wit of Emily Davies, the aristocratic directness of Lady Stanley ('Fools are so fatiguing', she once remarked at a dinner party) were replaced gradually by a kindly earnest spirit that found its fullest expression in the mistress-ship of Miss Constance Jones. She never failed to greet her students, even when she could think of nothing to say – 'Well, Miss Tarrant,' she once observed at a chance encounter, '*you* are going *up*stairs and *I* am coming *down*stairs.' Increasing athleticism rather disturbed her, but she adjured Miss Eleanor Duckett, 'If you *must* play hockey, hit the ball gently.'*

Hockey became really important; an Oxford match was played at Wimbledon 14 March 1894 and won by Cambridge by three goals; only one Oxonian 'sent a purler pop through the posts'. The ladies were rallied on their triumph in *Punch* by a parody of *The Battle of the Baltic*.

* The future Professor Tarrant of Bedford and Professor Duckett of Smith College, U.S.A.

Of the Battle of the Blues
  Sing a really martial strain,
When in particoloured hues
  Armed ladies took the plain
(With a fig for Mrs G. and her fads!)
  All in caps and dainty shirts,
  And emancipated skirts,
  And, as one report asserts,
    Ankle pads.★

Later, in Gwladys Jones, Girton gained an international player.

The first really masculine piece of organisation devised by Girtonians was the College Fire Brigade, founded by Sarah Marks in 1879, to endure for over half a century. Practices wet and dry were held, and strict discipline was imposed, the first members having been trained by Captain Shaw of the London Fire Brigade, celebrated in *Iolanthe*.

  O Captain Shaw,
    Type of true love kept under,
  Could thy Brigade, with cold cascade
    Quench my great love, I wonder?

Fortunately the members were never actually called upon to extinguish a fire, yet the Head Captain grew a most powerful figure in the College hierarchy; and this masculine game persisted into the nineteen-thirties, decades after the hoses were all leaking, and the Cambridge Fire Brigade had been mechanised.

By jesting about games, the gentlemen were able to defend more vital positions which were *not* being conceded, while the young ladies mistakenly but understandably seized on

★ Owen Seaman, *Horace at Cambridge*, p. 80.

the proffered role, and became more and more sporty. At first they had taken up gymnastics because it was thought that study would destroy their delicate frames; they continued with games in the valiant effort to be 'equal' in all respects, if hardly to 'distance' the men.

The Hockey Song, representing the Newnham Match in this popular sport, was sung to the tune of 'Knocked 'em in the Old Kent Road'; a student would even write to her fiancé with long accounts of sporting triumphs.*

In the rebellious nineties, the works of Ibsen, Bernard Shaw and Grant Allen were read, but the wider movement of 'revolting daughters' remained for Girtonians between the covers of books.

Mrs Warren's Profession, written in 1894, performed in 1902, makes a heroine of a Newnhamite who took third place among the Wranglers 'because the papers were full of Philippa Summers beating the Senior Wrangler'. Vivie Warren smokes cigars, drinks whisky, and aims at actuarial practice in London 'with an eye on the stock exchange'. Her mother, who had risen to the top of an older profession, is ruthlessly cast off by Miss Vivie – not without admiration for her talents; for though Vivie denounces such a way of life, she is won by Mrs Warren's defence: praise follows rebuke.

> Everybody has some choice, mother. The poorest girl alive may not be able to choose between being Queen of England or Principal of Newnham. But she can choose between rag-picking and flowerselling, according to her taste . . .

> My dear mother: you are a wonderful woman – you are stronger than all England. Are you really and truly not one wee bit doubtful – or – or – ashamed?

* See V. E. L. Brown, *The Silver Cord*, 1952. She came up in 1906.

Vivie freely admits the price she herself has had to pay for her achievement:

> Grind, grind, grind, for six to eight hours a day at nothing but mathematics ... outside mathematics, lawn-tennis, eating, sleeping, cycling and walking, I'm a more ignorant barbarian than any woman could possibly be who hadn't gone in for the Tripos.

Yet she sheds her lover with far less compunction than she does her mother, and the final curtain shows her happily submerged in her new employment.

> She goes buoyantly over to her place at the writing-table; pushes the electric lamp out of the way; pulls over a great sheaf of papers ... goes at her work with a plunge and soon becomes absorbed in her papers.

What actually occurred within college walls at Girton, perhaps even at Newnham, was much more conventional. As early as March 1886 it was resolved unanimously that the Browning Society at Girton should be dissolved, and its funds (1s. 7½d) spent on chocolates. How the gentlemen versifiers would have relished that item of news!

Formality of manners balanced private frolics; there was a strong sense of seniority and young ladies addressed each other as 'Miss So-and-so'; first names might be used only if the senior suggested it to the junior with the formula, 'May I prop?' Young Mary Clover, when she came up in 1895, promised her parents she would do nothing so 'fast' as to ride a bicycle, but on being tempted to this dangerous sport by a fellow student (Bertha Phillpotts), she was measured for a cycling skirt, with little elastic stirrups sewn into the hem to keep it down to the ankle. Of course the dangerous machine was stored in the college shed on Castle Hill, whence the rider proceeded decorously on foot. Her contemporary, young Alice Aitken, from a more conservative Scottish home, was offered the bribe of a hunter not to proceed to college where they seemed to be 'a fast lot'; she withstood the bribe.

By the turn of the century, Lady Dorothy Howard could plead – unsuccessfully – that supervisions should be held without the presence of a chaperon; more daringly and more successfully, that in amateur theatricals the students taking male parts should not be obliged to wear costumes 'draped to the knee'.

To such young women, who had led very sheltered lives, Girton gave the chance of mixing closely with girls of their own age from varied social backgrounds, for as the career of Sarah Marks reveals, students were never drawn exclusively from the girls' public schools; novels and stories of the time show the plight of the poor scholarship girl. In some cases their over-anxiety exposed them to great strain; differences of style, of entertainment, dress and deportment were certainly as acutely felt in a woman's college as in a man's. It was recorded by Miss Maynard that one Cambridge lady observed with relief after a dinner party, 'My dear, she was a nice girl, with rosy cheeks and nice manners and nicely dressed, and you wouldn't have thought she knew anything!'

The College commanded an undivided loyalty from its members. They still felt the exhilaration of opening up new careers for women as a result of their college years as each generation went out and became sanitary inspectors, or doctors, or missionaries in strange places, with the courage and confidence that deep security and prolonged education breeds. It was a good training, sharpening the wits and interests, while protecting the feelings and keeping the girls young for their years emotionally. The adventures of learning were enough. Many of these young women grew 'strong minded', while retaining all their lives a special attachment to the magic years. Those who stayed to teach devoted their lives to the place with unqualified fervour. After 1885, nearly all appointments at Girton and all appointments to the mistress-ship were from within. Indeed anything else would have been taken as a sign of the College's incapacity; even quite recently, very distinguished ladies have been apt to find that, in the eyes of the oldest members, twenty years' service did not quite compensate for the lack of those first three years.

The agony of appearing in the wrong place or the wrong clothes, the sting of a rebuke could remain for life. Mary Clover once coasted down the stairs of Middle Tower on a tea-tray, to land at the feet of the formidable Miss Jex Blake; and in her panic used the familiar nickname – 'I'm sorry, Miss Jix, I'm sorry, Miss Jix.' More than half a century later, as an old lady she told me the story, still shuddering at the memory.

An outsider's image of these times is preserved in the novels of L. T. Meade, which came out in the nineties – *The Girls of Merton College, A Sweet Girl Graduate* – essentially these are school stories with a college setting and do not differ greatly from the effusions of Miss Angela Brazil.

They depict in great detail the buildings, student customs and daily routine; there are, on the other hand, some very wild shots. 'Merton' possessed 'a gymnastics mistress' who coached the college boat. Perhaps the most extraordinary and revealing distortion is the portrait of the 'headmistress', Miss Jocelyn Silence. She was the product of a military family which brought forth male children only: 'Jocelyn was the first girl baby born into the family for a couple of hundred years.' At Cheltenham College she was told by Miss Beale that the noblest thing a women could do was to marry – or teach.

'Can she not do both?' asked Jocelyn.

'Perhaps,' replied Miss Beale; 'but I,' she said, and for a moment she looked sorrowful, 'have only had time for one'. [p. 44.]

From St Hilda's, 'that home of all homes for the intellectual girls of England', Jocelyn next proceeded to Merton; she was of course extremely beautiful 'with a full bust, a generous build of figure, finely developed broad shoulders' – for on them a good deal rested. The students presided over by this hermaphrodite were allowed mild flirtations, and the culmination of each book is a scene of mild amateur theatricals – in *A Sweet Girl Graduate*, a performance of *The Princess*, where the heroine is so moved by her part that she succumbs at once to the ardour of a Senior Wrangler.

The life of these excessively aesthetic young ladies was thought to range from sublime moments in King's College Chapel to a feminine preoccupation with the furnishing of their rooms – Watts' *Hope,* and Japanese lacquer tables – and to dressing becomingly. Penniless students, though requiring tactful treatment, and even the *parvenue*, most difficult of college girls, are succoured and helped; the crimes which carry forward a slender plot are of schoolgirl type – cheating in various forms, such as petty pilfering, or false claims to the authorship of a play.

Throughout the long afternoon of the Jubilee years and the reign of Edward VII, the college remained a closed society. Because of its early foundation, its size and comparative isolation, the individuality of Girton was pronounced. Rituals included late refreshments of 'Tray' and

'Jug'; the yearly cycle brought round its yearly events of Tripos teas and the Freshers' Rag – a fancy dress party; the little language and stock of college legends and songs accumulated, and built up a tradition powerful and conservative, though cosy and parochial. Different parts of the building acquired those names which lingered till the late twenties – Bear Pits, Boots, Slums, Loose Boxes, Rapids and the Taylor Knob.* E. M. List's *Girton, my Friend* (1905) describes a reading party at Sheringham, with all the personal nicknames – the Beauty, the Mighty One, and – in disarming innocence – the Honeymoon Couple.

Probably the life of the average student remained as restricted as that depicted by L. T. Meade. Gwen Raverat, daughter of the Darwins, recalls loftily

> the plop, plop, of the feet of the oldest horses in the world, as they plugged along, pulling the funereal cabs out to Girton with four melancholy students in each; while the drab Newnham girls skurried to and fro to their lectures on foot.†

This is the only notice that was ever bestowed on female undergraduates by that sharp-eyed young Edwardian Miss.

Protected by their chaperons, Girtonians might attend a few social functions; at first they were also chaperoned to lectures, for the late T. B. Allworthy, who married a Girtonian, told me that when he was an undergraduate in the late nineties, as the ladies entered with their escort, the class would rise politely to its feet. In the group he saw a girl with a particularly delicate beauty of complexion and colouring

* For the benefit of later generations, these names indicate Bottom Tower Wing, New Side, at first a closed corridor; the Surgery; the top floor over the Old Hall; the staircase at the end of Orchard Wing, the corner rooms at the junction of Orchard and Hospital Wings, given by Tom Taylor the dramatist in memory of his daughter.

† *Period Piece*, p. 45.

who was to spend a lifetime at Girton – Evelyn Cave-Browne-Cave. As an old lady, she still wrote college verses, invited students in to 'Jug', tended a small wild garden in which she planted bulbs that others discarded, her solitude cheered by a robin or a blackbird; and she remained so untouched by the world that to the end her expression was soft as a child's.

Indeed, Shaw's drama of the young rebellious Newnhamite might be contrasted with Grant Allen's story, *The Woman Who Did* (1895), where, if an advanced young woman were depicted as a daughter of the Church and a Girtonian it was but in order to let her protest against both the one and the other more effectually. Herminia Barton, daughter of the Dean of Didsbury, first appears dressed 'in a curious oriental navy-blue robe of some soft woollen stuff, a sort of sleeveless sacque embroidered in front with arabesques of gold thread' and confesses:

> I didn't take my degree. I didn't care for the life, I thought it cramping. You see, if we women ever are to be free, we must have a freeman's education. But the education at Girton only made a pretence of freedom. At heart, our girls were all as enslaved to convention as girls anywhere else. The whole object of our training was just to see how far you could manage to push a woman's education without the faintest degree of her emancipation.*

The young Oxonian in whom she confides is all assent – 'the pretended earnestness of these pallid Somerville girls is all an affectation of one-sided culture'. In the life of social and ethical emancipation which Herminia and this young man

---

* Grant Allen, *The Woman Who Did*, 1895, p. 45. This now almost forgotten book ran into several editions, and was reprinted after the First World War.

strenuously practise, it becomes clear that, as he had noticed, 'the iron of Girton had *not* entered into her soul'. The offspring of their union finds illegitimacy a handicap, and, to release her daughter from an unwanted tie, Herminia stages a dramatic deathbed scene. Clad in white, and wearing a simple nosegay, she unstoppers her little phial of prussic acid, which takes ten minutes to have its effect; such is the strength of an entirely emancipated woman.

Writers better acquainted with Cambridge than the author of *The Woman Who Did* make very little reference to the women's colleges. Neither Gwen Raverat nor E. M. Forster could penetrate the wall of gentility and social custom – or ever wished to, as it would appear. Not that their own society was much more free; Mrs Raverat describes

> the fantastic unreality of the outlook of decent people, from about 1850 to 1914 . . . For nearly seventy years the English middle classes were locked up in a great fortress of unreality and pretence; and no one who has not been brought up inside the fortress can guess how thick the walls were, or how little of the sky outside could be seen through the loopholes.*

By the turn of the century, the 'hot' area of feminist campaigning had moved back to women's suffrage. In the very year that Cambridge rejected admission of women, a Woman's Suffrage Bill reached a second reading in the House of Commons. Emily Davies had rejoined the Executive Committee of the National Society for Women's Suffrage in 1890, largely because as a non-militant she felt it necessary when 'a new and noisy section is apt to monopolise attention'. The moves for suffrage and for sexual emancipation were alienating conservative reformers; the

---

* *Period Piece*, p. 104. In fact the unconscious prejudice against the students is precisely an example of the barriers that Mrs Raverat is here alluding to.

days of hunger strike and of the Countess Markiewicz, M.P. were not too far ahead.* Far, far from Cambridge lay the not entirely imaginary adventures of H. G. Well's Ann Veronica, who went to jail as a suffragette, fell in love with a married lecturer in zoology at the University of London and pursued him to Switzerland. Emily Townshend, one of the original College Five, was a close friend of H. G. Wells, and at the Fabian Society championed his views against those of G. B. Shaw. She was also among the earliest supporters of D. H. Lawrence.

The First World War came to break up the 'long afternoon' and to change the image of feminine protest. Women gained the vote, and many social taboos were relaxed, not without contention between the generations. After the war, not only was there a renewed effort to obtain degrees, but a new set of social assumptions changed the daily lives of students.

A student's rebellion against the older generation, is conjoined with some naïve loftiness in Rosamond Lehmann's *Dusty Answer* (1927). The author was at Girton from 1919 to 1922, with the early post-war generation, and the shadow of the war lies across her story – older brothers have been killed, and young survivors are marked for life. Perhaps one third of the book is devoted to the heroine's life at Girton where the sensitive, intelligent, deeply introspective Judith is contrasted with a brilliant, sophisticated, volatile friend who absorbs her only to betray, when a dark, sinister woman of the world intervenes. But this, surprisingly enough, is precisely the story of *A Sweet Girl Graduate*. There is the same delight in a room of one's own, the same ineffable experience

* Countess Markiewicz, though the first woman actually elected to the House, refused to take her seat, but went there to see her name on a peg. She had been sentenced to death for her part in the Easter Rising in Ireland in 1916, and was elected while still in jail.

in King's College Chapel. A handsome male undergraduate (in Rosamond Lehmann's book, more than one) is ensnared by the heroine's charm.

But Miss Lehmann sets the ardour and beauty of the two heroines, almost inevitably named Judith and Jennifer at that date, against a sharp and mercilessly vivid portrait of a physically repulsive, anxious and unsuccessful scholarship girl, Mabel Fuller, with hungry and crypto-Lesbian affections. This girl, observed in a different way from any other character in the book, is at the opposite pole from the calm, endearing and passionate Mariella, whose illiterate and tragic confession resolves the plot. Something of Gwen Raverat's disdain for the College plodder appears; for Judith, of course, wins her dazzling 'First' in English, and Mabel, of course, a deserved oblivion.

The College group is both loved and hated; beyond the detested building and the enchanted garden, friendship at Granchester and betrayal at The Whim put the heroine at last into the Cambridge of Virginia Woolf, whose style is echoed in the slightly overpowering, but richly evocative set-pieces of nostalgia.

Jennifer was half asleep with her head upon the window-sill. The bowl of fruit burned in the dimness. How like Jennifer was her room! Yellow painted chairs, a red and blue rug on the hearth, cowslips in coloured bowls and jars, one branch of lilac in a tall blue vase; the guitar with its many ribbons lying on the table, a silken Italian shawl, embroidered with great rose and blue and yellow flowers flung over the screen; wherever you looked, colour leaped up at you . . .

'Now listen and we'll hear a nightingale. He's tuning up.' They leaned out of the window.

The icy aching flute in the cedar called and called on two

or three notes, uncertain, dissatisfied; then all at once found itself and bubbled over in rich and complicated rapture . . .

The end of the first year.   [pp. 158-9.]

'Oh, you're so good to me, you're so kind. And there's nothing I can do except hurt you. I've never done anything for you'.

'Oh, Jennifer, you've been all my happiness for two years.'

'It was very silly of you to be made happy by a person like me. You might have known I'd let you down in the end.'

'You haven't let me down'.

'Yes, I've made you unhappy.'

It was not much use denying that.   [p. 199.]

Sophistication and naïvety, arrogance and anxiety, unite in a story at once assured and yet touching, as a record more touching perhaps at fifty years' distance than at the time. For it shows the life of a woman's college as a setting less for intellectual than for emotional growth – a place which is to be taken entirely for granted, simply as environment. The social assumptions are sometimes ahead of the social structure depicted.

Demands of study no longer weigh heavily; obsolete rules no longer oppress, for the daring heroine goes for a long night drive with an undergraduate in his car, and afterwards brings him into her college room during Hall. This is, however, the full extent of her social emancipation; a hint of Lesbianism in the dark visitant from outside is kept muted. Betrayed by one friend after another, the heroine bids farewell to Cambridge with a sense of being rejected by the place itself – 'under its politeness, it had disliked and distrusted her and all other females'.

A year after the publication of *Dusty Answer*, the O.D.T.A.A. Society of Girton and Newnham invited Virginia Woolf to give a paper. It was this occasion which produced *A Room of One's Own*, in which the feminist case is put directly.*

Mrs Woolf contrasts the splendid lunch at a man's college with the dreary meal at a woman's. But I was told that the women's supper would have been better if Mrs Woolf had not sat so long looking at the sunset on the Backs that she came in long past the dinner-hour. On the other hand, the lunch in her honour had been exceptional; for even the most opulent men's college does not serve *crème brûlée* every day. We undergraduates enjoyed Mrs Woolf, but felt that her Cambridge was not ours.

College rituals had certainly declined; the College songs were forgotten. They were revived, as interesting Victoriana, after World War Two. Many ignored what chaperon rules still remained: it took some strong-mindedness to play games, unless you played them well.

Yet Gladys Crane, who came as a gyp to college in 1919 has recorded some surprising romps, that suggest the High School period was not over.

> We would sometimes have an apple-core thrown at us when you was walking along the corridor, but we would always aim back by throwing it through the ventilator over the top of the door, when they would run out after you and run you up the corridor.*

The Girton of the twenties was no longer a single community; there were school groups and school rooms as in the old days, there were others who boldly smoked Turkish cigarettes, cut lectures, and read *Ulysses*. It was an age of literary and philosophic excitement; but I remember, when

---

* 'I hope that your society is a great improvement on my sketch,' wrote Mrs Woolf to the Girton secretary, 29 January 1928 (in a letter preserved at Girton College).

* Jean Lindsay, *A Cambridge Scrapbook*, p. 68.

The vote of 1897. Cambridge rejects the admission of women

asked by Jacob Bronowski to contribute an article on the women's point of view to his magazine, *Experiment*, refusing with some emphasis, because I felt that a woman undergraduate should not have a different point of view. This was, perhaps, an over-emphatic 'protest' on my part.

Yet with the single community, the image of the Girton Girl had vanished. There are still novels dealing with Girton girls – Andrew Sinclair's *My friend Judas* (1959) has a Girton background, and the bright, sophisticated heroine who makes life so hard for the men undergraduates is not without her prototypes. Ancient prejudice and the ghost of an older idea of Girton is utilised in such a recent piece of sophistication as John Fowles's *The Magus* (1966). The *femme fatale* of this book presents herself at first as having read classics at Girton – she ends as the Trilby of a sinister magician. There are a few knowledgeable details just touched in: 'Miss Wainwright' the principal suggests that the author has at least consulted *Who's Who* to get a recognisable approach to first-hand knowledge. But Girton remains a symbol of lofty, disinterested learning, and its Mistress should really still have been Miss Jocelyn Silence.

The contending images can each be met. The bright, 'swinging' undergraduate can still make the national Press if she is elected President of the Union, but she must be feminine too. In the Antipodes I was told that some members of a Cambridge women's college still complained of a 'blue stocking' atmosphere; and when I retorted that blue aprons were the contemporary wear, this was recorded as news. Perhaps the subtle, and yet very powerful influence of Girton upon those who know it from within will some day find embodiment, not in news, entertainment or polemic but in a work of art. Meanwhile, never trust the image, trust the live encounter.

Part 3

A GENERAL VIEW

Chapter 6

THE COLLEGIATE UNIVERSITY
IN THE MODERN WORLD

I

THE story of Girton's second century will be part of the story of Cambridge University; of the new relations between university and colleges; between students and dons. For the rapid changes of our times, adaptability becomes the prime quality; our memories must not control our predictions.

Adaptability comes more readily through the comparison of different systems. Out of a small amount of personal knowledge and a pressing sense of personal need, I have attempted a first essay in comparative collegiate functions.

In the world of today, there is no single model for the university or the college, but there is an increasing sense that the academic society should 'feel small as it grows large'.* The concept of a 'cell' that is distinct but not divided from the larger community animates the advanced experiment of new collegiate campuses, recently established within the largest university in existence – Santa Cruz, and San Diego, the eighth and ninth centres for the university of California. Equally, it animates the newest universities of far less affluent governments, in the young societies of the Southern Hemisphere.

* This was Clark Kerr's definition of the campus at Santa Cruz, California.

Such experiments are the culmination of a long historic process; I make no apology, therefore, in this necessarily brief attempt to relate past and present, for passing rapidly over the early history of the older English universities – which is generally familiar – taking my main modern example from another English-speaking region and ending with illustrations from some collegiate universities founded, in the last few years, on the other side of the globe.

Freely to adapt an old guild statute, it might be hazarded that a medieval college was 'a group of persons, old and young, banded together in the service of learning, and prepared for the public attestation of their skill, who aim to live together in unity and care for each other as friends and companions'. By the *acta* of the German nation at Bologna, the oldest university of Europe, they agreed to 'mutual charity, mutual association and amity, the consolation of the sick and support of the needy, the conduct of funerals and the extirpation of rancour and quarrels, the attendance and escort of our doctorandi to and from their places of examination, and the spiritual advantages of members'.*

Some of these are openly and all of them are tacitly among the purposes of an Oxford or Cambridge college, although the term itself, as an honorific, is now applied to many institutions, from the Collegiate Church of St. Peter of Westminster, commonly called Westminster Abbey, to 'colleges' of beauty and hairdressing.

Graduation (complete with cap and gown) is a ceremony practised at American infant schools: while 'more than a

* Quoted from Hastings Rashdall, *The Universities of Europe in the Middle Ages*, Oxford 1936, Vol I, pp. 159–60.

dorm and less than a school' represents the attempt of one American newspaper to describe the College which had admitted Prince Charles.

In the past, colleges have appeared where there was some urgent and deeply felt need which a small group could satisfy. The first were houses of national groups in an international society of scholars; or local refuges for the members of international religious orders. Colleges appeared at Cambridge in numbers shortly after the Black Death had thinned the ranks of clerisy; others came two centuries later to spread the New Learning. Almost the only medieval clerical societies in England to be spared – indeed, augmented – by the royal yet predatory mandates of Henry VIII, colleges of the sixteenth century became not only centres of learning but of wealth, took a defined place within the newly emerging political societies of the time. A great French political philosopher of the Renaissance located them as intermediate between the 'community Natural' of the family and the 'community Civil' of the commonwealth or republic. According to Jean Bodin, rulers (such as Henry VIII and his successors) founded and maintained fraternities, communities and colleges

> to the end that the parts and members of the self-same body of a commonweal being at accord with themselves, it might be more easy to rule the whole commonweal together . . . for the unity, company and friendship they had among themselves, eating and drinking together for the most part and having no judge but themselves . . . knowing that amity and friendship was the only foundation of all humane and civil society and much more requisite for the keeping and maintaining thereof than justice itself for that justice . . . ends suits, but not hatred . . . whereas amity and friendship, which is by company

nourished, yielding the right of itself, best establisheth true and natural justice.*

If the great lawyer could make the concession of preferring 'harmonious justice' of the family to 'arithmetical justice' of the courts (his own terms), he thereby implies that collegiate form is bound to be self-regulating. Every college is distinct since it is shaped organically from within – and in fact, older colleges differ from each other to a surprising degree. However enlightened and liberal it may be, any external governing power reduces the collegiate standards of the institution it controls.

In the ancient universities of Aberdeen, Dublin and Durham, collegiate form differs widely from that of Oxford and Cambridge; at Harvard and Yale, the houses and colleges – though recently they have been more prominent – were for long periods relatively inconspicuous. The small size of the college unit allows this diversity and flexibility. At London, on the other hand, many of the colleges have reached the scale of universities in all but name.

A highly traditional society, governed largely by custom and agreement, though safeguarded by charters and statutes, needs constantly to be in touch with other societies. Not the independence but the closed system of college government led to the long stagnation of the eighteenth and early nineteenth centuries at Oxford and Cambridge. The corruption of the best produces the worst, and reform was to come only from without – with it a new burst of creative activity, resulting in the foundation of new colleges for these with

* Jean Bodin, *Six Books of a Commonwealth*, translated Richard Knolles (1605). Chapter VII, Book III, 'Of Corporations and Colleges, Estates and Communities', pp. 363–4. He adds that colleges may unite in a body politique or corporation, with the rights of a general community, as a university (p. 379).

special needs – working men, missionaries, and women.*
To the mid-nineteenth century period of reform belongs the
story of the first College for Women; its appearance followed
that of the girls' public schools, and so was part of another
great educational movement.

In any educational system, the universities, representing
the apex of growth, are not to be understood apart from the
preparatory stages of learning upon which they rest. The
universities of England, Scotland, Canada and the United
States, Australia and New Zealand differ in form as blossoms
that spring from different roots and are nourished in different
soils. In comparing the one with the other, it must not be
assumed that there is a single structure which may be called a
'university'. In practice, the universities themselves accept
pragmatic distinctions (e.g. for the purposes of affiliation)
ranging from the universities of the 'world class' to those
that merely utilise the titles and formalities of higher learning. Commercial interests or misplaced national pride
(universities are as essential as airlines to national prestige)
may command that bread may be made of stones; while
continuing to call it bread.

The new international relation of universities with each
other is far more tenuous and precarious than the relations
of each with its local educational environment. That growth
of natural science, which from the end of last century has
gradually led to the centralising of power at university level
in Oxford and Cambridge, has rendered these places dependent on Government finance; and this, in turn, limits
international affiliations that learning in itself develops.

Since the Second World War, jet travel has made it possible for professors to fly the Atlantic for brief conferences –

* See the various works of D. A. Winstanley, *Unreformed Cambridge*,
1935, *Early Victorian Cambridge,* 1940, and *Later Victorian Cambridge*, 1947.

even, occasionally, to hold official positions on both sides simultaneously and to commute. Young students, too, become world travellers by jeep or charter flights; the fashions of Telegraph Avenue and King's Parade repeat each other and, in the Long Vacation, special flights to Australia convert British students to 'instant Jackaroos'. But internationalism is not always of first interest to government, as the plan for raising of fees for overseas students in British universities has proved. 'At one time', said a colonial official sadly to me, 'if there were a local revolution, you could be fairly sure the leader had been at Oxford or Cambridge *and* in the local jail. Today it's no longer so'.

The mid-nineteenth century saw the older colleges reach close relations with the public schools, since both were engaged in training up young men for a clear national purpose – to serve as colonial administrators, lawyers or doctors, civil servants or clerics.* The social revolution of the mid-twentieth century requires that colleges reshape themselves, and expand to meet the new forms of educational community. Perhaps, since the international society has returned, they also should return to their medieval roots. Relatively speaking, they are once again communities of poor scholars; the college may still have silver plate, but it can rarely afford to supply typists.†

In our mobile community, the 'unity, company and friendship' of a college offers special opportunities to the visiting stranger. The president of a great college for women in America recently said:

* See Sheldon Rothblatt, *The Revolution of the Dons*, 1968.

† The head of one of the richer colleges, who in his Reith Lectures expressed a feeling of nothing but contempt for history, might be reminded of I. A. Richards' 'Contempt is a well-known defensive reaction'.

THE COLLEGIATE UNIVERSITY

The administrator, as I see him, must be a kind of Socrates, wandering about the capitals of the academic world, and asking the hurrying faculty what they mean by truth, justice, decency, even academic freedom. And he must ask the students why they learn so well what they maintain is useless and what they mean by integrity and how they recognise it and above all what they think is going on . . . the university is the place where discussion between generations is still possible.*

In a college, it may be added, Socrates can put his questions and receive his answers more searchingly and quickly than elsewhere.

Recently, in a visit to a far distant university, where controversial views on English studies have developed, I was officially asked to address a seminar, at which senior members were present and innocuous subjects discussed. But just before, while lunching at one of the colleges, I was told that the students, that very afternoon, were staging a protest meeting against the syllabus. Only in a college could a stranger expect to arrive with such promptitude at the full state of affairs.

By cutting across the official and often very powerful divisions of academic life, the 'unity, amity and company' of college life gains special value at this time. It is not to the interest of colleges that they should become completely identified with the already existing power divisions – whether on a faculty basis, or to represent the vertical division between undergraduate and graduate students. The college must expect rather to be a centre of protest, of discussion, of conflicting views, within a framework of tolerance and acceptance. In an open society, the small group protects individuality and maintains qualitative against quantitative

* Rosemary Park, former Principal of Barnard College, now Vice-Chancellor at Los Angeles; in a speech at Pasadena, 23 February 1967.

standards; and, as in medieval times, it may still serve to 'extinguish rancours and quarrels' – for brilliant minds are inevitably difficult minds! The most ominous and darkly spreading area of rancour and quarrel, however, no longer lies between faculty and faculty but between generation and generation. This offers special opportunities to take up a new function, which, if the colleges have vision to see it, may prove as valuable as any past achievements.

Working on a small scale, and in personal ways, a college remains not only the best instrument of the higher education, but the best remedy against our present conflicts. As a centre for discussion between generations, the college is free from those professional pressures which become so obvious in a faculty group. It might be argued of course, that if this principle is adopted, colleges should be totally without bias or special interest, and more particularly that they should be co-educational.

Without at this point discussing further the role played by women's colleges in the modern world, it may be observed in passing that Girton, which was founded to establish the right of women to the same intellectual training as men, may discover a further duty to protect the special interests of women within a university where, being at last accepted as full members, they begin to consider the differentiating aspects of their intellectual life rather than those they share with men.*

The separate college for women maintains the existing structure of separate schools for girls, and should these disappear, of course, its position would be weakened. Academic freedom is now most seriously threatened by the pressures

* See Chapter 4, pp. 79-80 Women have long been used to the irrational hostility that at present in university life is directed against quite other objects.

from the 'commonweal' which might well obliterate the 'family' aspects of academic life. The cost of maintaining a university is such that it must be dependent on public funds – but as the medieval guild protected its scholars against an ecclesiastical bureaucracy (*ad cathedram non pertinet studentium societas!*) so colleges may act as bulwarks against take-over by a national bureaucracy, with its risk of learning being subordinated to doctrinaire social planning. The collegiate structure of the University of Ghana is said to have helped in the struggle against Kwame Nkrumah's control; this gave its 'cells' the protection of being able to act both separately and collectively.

In U.S.A., Regents who control the State universities may in their local projects conflict both with the community of scholars and the Federal Government. In Canada, the two cultures of French and English both stimulate and also limit progress; and, as in Australia, rivalry between provincial Governments makes transition from one university to another a difficult matter. In England, State control has been held back by traditions of delegation and self-government long established in the older universities. If the academic community enjoys a higher degree of self-determination than anywhere else in the world, collegiate form embodies and safeguards this position most conspicuously.

Yet, although the new universities, York, Lancaster and Kent, have adopted the college system, it is more common to find alternatives proposed. In Cambridge, to a larger extent than at Oxford, sniping at colleges is a main resource of university journalists. A don suggests that the Master's Lodge be transferred to use by a faculty, and refers to colleges as 'halls of residence' (even 'subsidised canteens').*

* See the article by Jack Goody, 'Is your Master really necessary?' *The Cambridge Review*, 22 April 1967.

Yet at the same time, old non-collegiate institutions in both Oxford and Cambridge have assumed college status, while new societies appear in greater numbers than at any time since the Renaissance. College lodgings are no longer available and more undergraduates move into college rooms. Married quarters for research students are being built, and in one graduate college the whole family is admitted to a cafeteria lunch.

'Shock Report slams the Tutors', shrieks a headline in the students' weekly; while underneath in small type it is confessed, 'but only 15 per cent said they were not proud to be Johnsmen'. From the Antipodes comes a student lament for lack of 'student-staff political groups, faculty and subject societies, student writing and publishing, protest meetings' – as if these last were a form of social intercourse, which, in point of fact, they are. A student who knows he will have to go out to face a world indifferent and vast prepares himself for conflict in an environment which he believes not to be entirely hostile. It is because he assumes the essential friendliness of his seniors that he can afford to rage, and see how far he can go – a process known in America as 'testing out the administration'. There, of course, teachers and administrators being more sharply distinguished species, he may call on the first to support him against the second.

In England, students tend to state their case in the language of the larger society; thus, a demand for a single common room for senior members and graduate students is advocated as 'integration' – it implies, of course, apartheid for undergraduates. A Californian student writes 'Notes from a County Jail' sure of social approval and achieves publication in *The New York Review of Books* (15 Feb. 1968).

Undergraduates are prepared to condemn as 'apathy' the

absence of protests (which in more positive terms could be interpreted as content), modelling their stance on that of W. S. Gilbert's British Tar:

His foot should stamp, and his breast protrude,
And this should be his customary attitude.

Anticipation of hostility reached its strongest form in a leaflet which I picked up in the library of the University of Sydney during the recent conflict; 'Don't keep this', it warned, 'or you'll be arrested.'

The university library at Sydney offers the most valuable amenities that great centre has enjoyed for many years – some of the features of a college or a club. Besides housing the finest university library in the land, it is designed with all care to provide 'browsing areas', rooms for discussion, music rooms, the whole equipment for a student's day. Yet because library fines for late return of books were increased without prior notice (a penalty easily avoided) students staged a 'sit-in' during 1967, which inflicted some damage, and strained public relations even more. It was as though they felt the need to attack what they most deeply needed because they wanted more; while, at the same time gleefully suggesting, 'We'll have a ball in the library tonight!'

Conflict between the 'Community Natural' and 'Community Civil' may be further traced in that apparent inconsistency which drives some junior members to demand adult status within the community and simultaneously the kind of personal and individual attention from their teachers which is due to a favourite son. Paternalism is rejected and in a society where family ties have weakened, the remains of paternalism in tutorial authority is to be found chiefly in students' recognition of their prime right and duty to assert adult status by quarrelling with father.

The Provost of King's, who denounced family life in his Reith Lectures for 1968, presides over a college which expends much thought and time on consulting its undergraduates and maintaining a personal connexion between senior and junior members. On the other hand, those who object to the college as the obsolete survival of a system designed to educate a small *élite* for imperial rule would replace it by the equally obsolete system of the nineteenth century Trade Unions, a highly conservative and sometimes an impeding element in social structure. Or rather they would superimpose this on such elements of the present system as appeal to or are taken for granted by those who enjoy them.*

It may be that the younger generation, feeling deeply deprived by the rapid changes of modern society, and the uncertain future which greater conflicts impose, do not think the experience of age will any longer prove of relevance to themselves in ordering their own lives. 'We don't want our elders to tell us what to do' – because, it is felt, they can't possibly know. The support and protection of experience, the wisdom of the tribe, becomes irrelevant if in twenty years the tribe may have emigrated to the moon. No longer can old men or women of the tribe claim that kind of authority which the normal pace of evolution has hitherto conferred; hence the lost, resentful solidarity of youth.

Although there is a habit of terming senior members 'the authorities' power is recognised, but authority, the personal concomitant, is not.

Power relations being always potentially conflict relations, and entry to the older universities highly competitive, the energy and aggression that is achieved is directed on to the

* This provides an ironic comment on the remark of Clark Kerr that 'the university and segments of industry are growing more alike'.

next stage of attainment, and on to its nearest representatives. 'Student power' is in fantasy achieved in student protests which are perpetually 'hitting out', 'rocking', 'slamming' or 'shocking' somebody. The electric metaphor is sustained in the milder demand for more 'contacts with dons'; this combination of intimacy and impersonality suggests the meeting of strangers and the transmission of some power current. The proffer of the family relation, one built on shared assumptions, nourished by the deep soil of common habits, may be rejected with great indignation as a piece of hypocrisy.

Yet the image of the university as factory is rejected with even more indignation.

Attacks on Presidents and the recipients of honorary degrees are sometimes quite openly attacks on father. For years, President Kerr was the object of particular attention from Berkeley students; Hal Draper's *The Mind of Clark Kerr* presented him as the advocate of the impersonal University Factory. When, however, in the struggle over tuition fees he was so unceremoniously and instantly stripped of office, he underwent a metamorphosis. The first howl of execration 'Good riddance to bad rubbish' was withdrawn with apologies, and the activist leader stated, 'He's a father, if a bad father.' Now, he is invited to address graduands and has become an accepted hero.*

This is the role to which most senior members must adopt themselves; skill to interpret Angry Rhetoric is perhaps now a first lesson in the modern Trivium. It must be always taken seriously; but not always literally.

* In 1968 he delivered the Marshall Lectures at Cambridge and was so successful in dealing with questioners that he reduced a potentially unpleasant situation to coolness. One student cited Herbert Marcuse's *Repressive Tolerance!*

II

In any account of the higher education of women, it is fitting that the Americans should earn first mention, for in this respect they led the rest of the English-speaking world. Mount Holyoke (1837), Emily Dickinson's college, started as a seminary, four years after the first beginnings of Oberlin Collegiate Institute; but Vassar College, in 1865, began with a course designed to equal that of the best men's colleges.

Before the foundation of English colleges, Sophia Jex-Blake had written her *Account of a Visit to Some American Schools and Colleges* (1867) and Barbara Bodichon, one of the founders of Girton, had also visited widely in U.S.A.* A graduate of Yale, the Rev. Henry Durant, who shared in the founding of Wellesley, went West to the new state of California, where – in the years that the College for Women opened in England – he was to lay the first foundations of the largest single enterprise of higher education in the world.

The University of California experienced from the first that struggle between individual claims and social demands, between private ideals, and State control which preoccupies educationalists today. In the highly dramatic story of this great university, incidents both of academic courage, and of violence reveal the issues with exceptional clarity. Contemporary problems, including those which have in Britain as yet not fully emerged, can already be discerned in California, 'wave of the future'; the form of its student protest has been widely imitated in England and elsewhere. I have therefore chosen it as my main example of the relations of college and university in the modern world.

* See Chapter I. p. 23.

Its inceptive body was a small liberal and ecumenical private foundation, the work of two New England clerics – a Congregationalist from Dartmouth, and a Presbyterian from Yale. In 1853, very soon after the forty-niners had opened up the Golden West with a rush, this Academy started in Oakland at a relatively safe distance from the big bad city of San Francisco; even so, the Rev. Henry Durant, first Principal, found that the domestic supervisor of his dormitory had put up a shingle advertising the place as a general boarding-house, with liquor for sale within. This worthy felt that 'whatever did not succeed in California within two and half months, would never succeed'; when Durant tried to eject him, he first offered bodily violence, but, on the sudden, turning deathly pale, lowered his fists and began to pray.

'I suppose,' said President Gilman, to whom Durant in old age told the story, 'he had a sudden vision of the future glories of the University of California.'

The college site had to be protected from 'jumpers' by a 'respectable fence', and later the Principal took possession of the half-completed building and defended it from an attempt at take-over by the contractors, his ultimate deterrent an axe half-concealed beneath his bed. Durant, who had been described as 'not suspicious and not severe enough to manage naughty boys – he would succeed admirably, I would think, in a female seminary', had a winning way, but he failed to win Governor Haight when in 1868, the College of California merged with a new State University. Haight admitted the value of the beautiful new Berkeley site, but disapproved of the college's weight of debts. 'Its aims were lofty', he declared, 'its men to be revered, but it had not got there' – and privately added, 'These gentlemen expected to have a good deal to say about the organising of the University; but I'll see that they don't.'*

The new university, holding as its primary purpose the founding of a school of agriculture and mines, was practical and secular in its design; so, only after a lengthy search for a President – which included such surprising candidates as General McClellan – did the Governor and Regents accept the Rev. Henry Durant. Berkeley still gives the name of Agricultural Hall to one building to meet the conditions of its incorporation.

In the same university term that women first appeared in the vicinity of the University of Cambridge, the University of California admitted its first students; in the following year 1870, women appeared in California also. Among the first was the editor of the campus newspaper, who evidently looked forward to a life that, if strenuous, would be yet tranquil. Miss Josephine Lindley declared earnestly, in words that would have found an echo across the Atlantic:

> Every young lady should be fitted to *do* something in life. Too many of this period are raised in extravagance and care only for the superficial glitter of an easy, exciting life . . . the fate of young women's attempt in California to reach a higher, more real education depends on this experiment.†

Henry Durant's 'Twelve Apostles', his first graduates, maintained the tradition of a small liberal arts college; and almost until the end of the century his university grew very slowly. Throughout its history, the conflict between State control and individual assertions of freedom had been pre-

* See William Walter Ferrier, *Origin and Development of the University of California*, Berkeley, 1930, Part III, Chapter XX, p. 297.

† *The University Echo*, March 1871. Quoted by Ferrier, pp. 332-3. Miss Lindley ignores Mills College (founded 1865) which still remains as a college for women.

sent; yet, with the sudden giant growth of recent years, both have intensified.

Recent events have shown the power of State control. After a change of Government, the budget was ruthlessly slashed, and in January 1967 the Regents summarily dismissed the President of the University. In the previous month, when a number of graduate assistants had sympathised with a student strike, the Regents sent out a notice to all staff, high and low, deploring this behaviour as contrary to the highest standards of academic life; moreover (the notice continued), the Regents were advised it was illegal, and therefore anyone repeating the action in future would be liable to penalties, including dismissal.

Appeals to lofty sentiment that turn into orders for hired 'hands' may have represented a division of opinion in the body of Regents, but illustrate also the tension of two concepts, the private and the public forms of education. American scholars believe that the existence of both kinds of university acts as a safeguard of standards – the private universities have to pay competitive stipends, the public universities cannot become too bureaucratic. Before the founding of the University of California, one hopeful politician declared:

> If we have the means, we can procure the necessary talent; we can bring the President of Oxford University here by offering sufficient salary!

On the other hand, the private founders of the College of California had felt that

> the State university becomes of course a mere prize for placemen and subject to all the contests, agitations, and changes of party politics . . . the faculty come in at the same gate with the

constables and the marshals . . . Meanwhile the students are rushing into some cabal or party to oust some obnoxious President or Professor, and he, on the other hand, is called upon to administer the discipline in peril of a retaliatory discipline that takes away his bread.*

These words, written in 1856, became newly applicable in 1966.

A second campus of the university developed in 1919 and by 1929 was fully established at Los Angeles; by 1937 seven centres, and to day nine (each the equivalent of a modern European university) now absorb 88,000 students.

In 1966 the university budget of California at $650,000,000 exceeded the total revenue of many modern states.

This great complex body is planned to relate to the total educational structure; the 'State colleges' – originally teachers' training colleges – are on the way to becoming State universities with junior colleges acting as feeds; many private institutions to supplement the work.

The University of California may become largely postgraduate – or at least 50 per cent postgraduate, which is the percentage at the small influential private California Institute of Technology.

The most affluent State of the most affluent country in the world still offers education to native Californians at a very low cost;† however, that starry galaxy of Nobel Prizemen

---

* William Walter Ferrier, *Ninety Years of Education in California*, pp. 311–2. The statement was made by Horace Bushell, who came to survey the prospects in 1856.

† For a Californian, incidental fees cost about $300 a year. In August 1967 the Regents rejected a proposal to establish tuition fees, but other fees were raised in 1968. Non Californians pay a very much higher rate.

who adorn the leading campuses of the university are not as a rule engaged in teaching. It is said that at Berkeley, 60 per cent of the instruction for undergraduates is given by graduate assistants – that is, by research students. If, as one of the most admired of the American radical educationalists has said,

> The culture of the scholars is inevitably foreign; it is international, and comprises the past, present, and future,

Paul Goodman's words apply at present only to the most senior members of the group.

On the contrary, the concept of the 'Multiversity' which President Kerr put forward for California, implies that the University should be prepared to serve the professional and industrial needs of the community, as its first political founders intended. This evokes a mood of alienation and revolt among students, who feel inexorably moulded by social pressure – in a supposedly free society – towards an end which disregards them; as the student leader of 1964, Mario Savio, declared: 'They must suppress their most creative impulses; this is the prior condition for being part of the system'. The University becomes a machine for maintaining conformity in 'the Utopia of automated, sterilised contentment'. In one student demonstration, a placard was borne which read: 'I am a student of the University of California; do not fold, bend or mutilate.'

Clark Kerr admitted that big State universities are the most vulnerable to the charge of neglecting students.* The affluent society produces the beggar's uniform of dirty sweaters. Californian 'sit-ins' provided a model for students all over the world. Paradoxically, social planning produces

---

* In *The Uses of the University*, Harvard 1963. Quoted Lipset and Wolin, p. 45 (see following footnote.)

disorder as the expansion of education leads to a feeling of frustration and a sense of neglect, whether in Berkeley or Berlin or Britain.

When, after a series of incidents in the autumn of 1964, the Riot Squad of Alameda County removed hundreds of Berkeley students from the Administration Building, where they were staging a sit-in, to Santa Rosa 'correctional facility' (Californian for 'jail'), this 'Day of the Cops' passed into mythology.*

It was a student triumph. The university had no easy informal means of dealing with students' problems at the personal level, and the faculty members rushed to bail out their pupils. Two years later, however, a new strike movement failed to win academic support, but the student 'activists' adroitly turned failure into jest by appearing at a masked ball as hippies, 'Friends of the Lone Star Ranger'.

Both activists and anarchists of California have provided a model for European students. Hipsters of San Francisco who live their lives unhooked from society, and sometimes hooked on psychedelic drugs, regard Berkeley as their home ground; for a State university is treated as public property, culturally open to any international Bohemian drawn to San Francisco, one of the most beautiful cities in the world. The result sometimes feels as if the Orators' Corner from Hyde Park had been set down in the court of London University. All extra-curricular life is open to 'non-students'.

In Oxford and Cambridge the 'fringe' is provided by the

* Clark Kerr, in a speech at Cambridge, indicated that the Governor of California gave this order. For an account of the events see *The Berkeley Student Revolt, Facts and Interpretations*, a collection of contemporary documents edited by Semour Martin Lupset and Sheldon H. Wolin, Doubleday, 1965, p. 165. See also the book edited by Seymour Martin Lupset, *Student Politics*, New York, 1967, for a comparative study, including Latin America, India, and African universities.

'language schools' for foreign students, and various auxiliary educational bodies which make use of the prestige that attaches to these seats of learning.

Looking at California, a sociologist from the eastern States said wistfully, 'They're both hippy and square' – but a sterner voice denounced the undergraduate career as 'a four-year course in sex, drugs, and treason'.

Dr Timothy Leary, founder of the League for Spiritual Discovery, proposed to use hallucinatory chemicals as 'a sacrament', while a Berkeley schoolboy, charged with the possession of 'pot', said he knew it was 'a hang-up', but 'he owed it to himself to enlarge his consciousness'.

Thus the Protestant Ethic may be enlisted in the cause of disaffiliation.

In California everything may be simulated, and sometimes there is little power to distinguish between the original and the reproduction – 'authentic' Spanish, Japanese, Mexican restaurants will attract everyone except the Spanish, Japanese or Mexicans. There is, too, a lack of commitment which comes from the memory of the old Frontier – so succinctly voiced to Durant by the lodging-house keeper. Then, too, climate changes quickly over the Bay.

It was, however, neither simulation nor change of climate which led the great university to revert to the model of its inceptive college, and in 1965 to found two new collegiate campuses. Santa Cruz and San Diego revived the ideals of Henry Durant.

The expanding university had realised the need to decentralise; it was now planning to combine the advantages of a small liberal arts college with the resources of a great university. The new campus at Santa Cruz based its college structures on the model of Oxford and Cambridge – the aim avowed that the campus shall 'feel small as it grows large'. The State provided a site beautifully and conveniently distanced from the big bad city, libraries and labs, students' hostels. These colleges are dependent on private benefactions for such necessities as a Provost's house, a college library, senior common room, funds for welfare and for entertainment; already the distinction between rich and poor has appeared, not inevitably to the disadvantage of the poorer colleges.

They differ from the colleges of an English university in having some variations in their curriculum – for lower division only at Santa Cruz, for the full course at San Diego.

In this return to an old model as the answer to a problem that is universally felt, salutary lessons emerge for the proponents of what has been termed in America 'the shoddy revolution in British education'.★

In some respects, of course, there is a time-lag. Californian colleges are co-educational but the residents' houses are not, and at Santa Cruz 'intervisitation' is restricted to the public rooms. This has aroused vehement student protest, which even the proximity of the redwood forest cannot charm away.

'How wonderful to sit under these redwood trees and read Shakespeare,' said a prospective girl student with a sigh of satisfaction.

'Yes, the forest of Arden,' I replied, 'You may find Orlando has dropped beside you, like an acorn from an oak tree.'

★ Derek Colville, *The Yale Review*, Spring 1965 – a trenchant indictment of our present educational trends.

Mamma looked severe.

'I have heard,' she said sharply, 'that these woods are full of poison ivy.'

As the State universities try to incorporate the virtues of the private colleges, so the private colleges are tending to develop a 'cluster system' which allows them to pool resources for more costly requirements – such as laboratories – and to exchange teachers. In California, the well-established Clairmont group now consists of five associated graduate or undergraduate colleges; this cluster system has developed also in the Connecticut river valley; in Minneapolis – St. Paul, I found a group of religious foundations – Roman, Presbyterian and others – who had reached a very satisfactory exchange system.

Among the leading women's colleges of the 'seven Sisters' group, Vassar had planned an alliance with Yale, which involved moving the entire institution. I was told students and faculty were strongly in favour of this, and even the administration were fairly keen; but the plan has been shelved. Smith College has joined a local cluster, Wellesley has allied itself with M.I.T.

These joint enterprises may each produce a different relation of the associated colleges. Sometimes in older associate groups, co-operation releases more energy for new enterprise, such as the experiment with graduate women's re-employment at Radcliffe College. No American college known to me enjoys the full liberty of academic self-government that constitutes the tradition at Oxford and Cambridge; 'the Board' or 'the Trustees' have the last word.

III

An even more limited autonomy is imposed by State or Federal control on the newly founded collegiate universities in the Southern Hemisphere – the Australian National University at Canberra, Flinders at Adelaide and La Trobe at Melbourne.*

Australia's first universities were established before those of California, though also in a pioneer community. The home base was much farther away, the private contributions less considerable. Australia even yet is not an outstandingly affluent society, yet this country of $11\frac{1}{2}$ million now contains fourteen universities – while New Zealand, with a population of $2\frac{1}{2}$ million, has six.

The educational pyramid presents a steep slope, however; but the gradient comes *within* the university. The claim to ready admission is hotly defended as a democratic right, even though it means, as one harassed professor observed, 'I'm running a junior college, in the first year.' Failure and drop-out rate after one year is in some subjects as high as 50 per cent. Four-year courses lead for the most part to a pass degree; relatively few take honours; with advanced studies yet rarer. While the best students can be matched against any in the world, there remains the fact that 2,000 English students in the first year may dwindle to something like 100 for honours finals; these numbers mean that nearly all the junior teaching must be delegated to assistants. Instruction is imparted, as it were, from a very high

* One of the most complete accounts of the Australian Universities is *Tertiary Education in Australia*; a report submitted by a committee under the Chairmanship of Sir Leslie Martin to the Commonwealth Government (1964); see also F. J. Schonell *et al. Promise and Performance*; a study of student progress at University level. (Brisbane, 1962.)

dais – sometimes, perhaps, through a loud speaker system.

The oldest universities – Melbourne for instance – still conduct correspondence courses with the country parts; and there is always a large group of extra-mural students.

A particularly loose and indefinite form of association therefore characterises these universities. Physically the first, Sydney (1850) and Melbourne (1853), are modelled on Oxford and Cambridge; the Great Hall at Sydney, with its Oxford and Cambridge windows, symbolises the early ideals, though with all the sun of that more generous clime caught in its warm yellow stone. Round what remain of the grass courts, scholars still hurry in black gowns: but the syllabus was modelled on the Scottish universities, crossed now with some features of the American 'credit' system: round the periphery cling a few small colleges, created as religious foundations to supply what an aggressively secular foundation omitted.

Here may be seen the first strata of a system of mass education that began under severe handicaps. After the Second World War, air travel within a short space of time transformed the Australian communities from their extreme isolation and loneliness – strung out round the periphery of a territory vaster than the United States, but lacking the firm ideological cement that joined the Puritans of New England or the revolutionaries of 1786. (Australia has been called six islands; each capital is isolated from the rest by great desert reaches, as barren as the bottom of the sea – which, not long ago geologically, some of them were.)

The egalitarianism of early settlers did not lead to that sort of movement which in the North of England created the Mechanics' Institutes and Penny Readings; education was at first a commodity to be supplied by men trained to educate, rather than a social function.

A GENERAL VIEW

By the mid-sixties of this century, the first two universities were crowded into island sites, each at the heart of a great sprawling capital city stretching out in area to rival Greater London or even Los Angeles. There are about 16,000 students at Sydney and at Melbourne, where highly unpopular quota systems regulate admission. In other capital cities, the various State universities are facing the problem of moving from central sites or establishing outlying colleges, which eventually become independent.

After the Second World War, the Commonwealth itself established the Australian National University at Canberra, an *élite* postgraduate institution devoted to such limited fields of national importance as, for example, medicine or Pacific Studies. A small university compared with others it has been accused of 'poaching'. Provincial Governments, not without a spice of local rivalry, retain regional control of all other establishments. Very recently, feeling that lack of undergraduate studies is a weakness, A.N.U. has absorbed Canberra University College as its school of general studies, and now provides residential colleges for both graduates and undergraduates.*

A move towards centralisation in a decentralised country, the fully collegiate university is here decidedly an innovation. The majority of Australian students live at home, though the older universities retain some small colleges holding between a hundred and two hundred students apiece; so that private collegiate structure remains as a minor modification of a monolithic structure. Such colleges now supply general tutorial aid to their students, who yet form a very small proportion of the whole.

The ideal that education should be available for all who

* In 1968 it provided Cambridge University with its first Professor of Sociology.

wished to try, but that it could be achieved on a do-it-yourself basis, went with a bent towards science and technology. University classes grew larger and larger, and sometimes lectures were relayed or held in double shifts; in short, many of the newer megalithic features of California could have been paralleled in Australia, twenty years ago.

A second creation promoted the Universities of New South Wales at Sydney, and Monash at Melbourne. The streamlined buildings of glass, concrete and brick, functional, have been filled with bright irreverent students, prepared also to campaign against the Government on such issues as war and capital punishment, to explode the sacred myths of the tribe. At 'Kenso High' or 'the Tech' (New South Wales started as a technical college) the staff at one time clocked in; Monash ('The Farm') has achieved a rapid growth that is the envy of other places.

Yet even these new growths did not meet all needs, and a third stage can be seen with the founding of Macquarrie at Sydney (1966), La Trobe at Melbourne (1966), and a second university, Flinders, at Adelaide (1965).

In at least two of these may be found some elements of the new Pacific educational community, for they are planned as residential collegiate universities, on the same pattern as the new campuses of California. Flinders bears indeed some physical likeness, in its siting, to Santa Cruz. The new Californian campuses supplied their library plans as a basis for the Australian venture; the first honorary degree from Santa Cruz went to Sir Robert Menzies.

In less happy and less deliberate imitation, the new Australian campuses have fallen victims of Government economies at their inception. La Trobe and Flinders are never-the-less rapidly expanding their intake and it is doubtful if

147

the residential scheme can immediately proceed on its original generous scale. (In Australia, the tradition of private benefaction has not yet been established to compensate for Government economy.) A second university planned for Queensland has been postponed; Tasmania voted against the proposal for a second university till Hobart exceeded 5,000 students; at Perth, in the most rapidly expanding of all Australian states, the only free university in the Commonwealth still counts only 4,500. It seems therefore that hitherto rapid growth may slow down for a while.

But, in the same way as the new Sydney University Library provoked student attention, existing colleges, which would seem to be the logical answer to Australian difficulties, may encounter student hostility. An angry 'activist' in New South Wales has attacked them because they lead to 'apathy' and

fragment any possible campus unity and community into small units which become absorbed in their internal affairs and parochial competition – a feature also of New England [i.e. the University of New England at Armidale] where 87 per cent of full-time students are in college . . . they prolong in many cases the atmosphere and attitudes of school life – particularly boarding-school life . . . they give none of the advantages of the originals on which they were supposed to be modelled, the colleges of Oxford and Cambridge . . . College meals draw students away from important meetings . . . Nonconformity does not go over well with college officialdom or its members . . .*

*The University Student '67, Current Affairs Bulletin published by the Department of Adult Education in the University of Sydney, Vol. 39, No. 8, March 13 1967, p. 117.

With no sense of incongruity, the same writer observes that the majority of students, living at home, also suffer from 'prolonged adolescence'; that students belonging to clubs or societies are more frequently the college residents – which is natural, because of transport problems. He ends with a proposal for high-density campuses, to include halls of residence with cafeterias, hygienically divested of all 'college spirit'.*

Australia, a beautiful empty land, has had gradually to seek its own identity; the city of Canberra which itself represents such a search, has recently found itself, and begun spontaneously to expand. Universities too reflect something of this search in their successive forms. The family is still a most powerful social influence in Australia – the need for separate small homes, each with its garden plot, has produced the great sprawl of Australian cities. General social life remains easy and informal – based on picnics and race meetings, long days at the beach, the Returned Soldiers' League, the sports club. Improvised, casual, such life may mask an essential apartness. Students are either quiet and shy, or dramatically in revolt against the old solidarities of the Church and Anzac Day ('The One Day of the Year' has been the subject of a satirical play).

The regular life of a small community that is also a cell of a larger community runs therefore directly contrary to Australian custom and habit; any new collegiate centres must be modified accordingly. Yet residential college life offers none the less an obvious if a costly solution to some local problems. Women have not, until recently, taken a prominent part in Australian professional life; but now women's

* Ibid, pp. 118, 127, 128. I have mentioned that it was in a hall of residence that I personally met student revolt at its promptest (see above, p. 127.)

halls of residence are opened at Melbourne, Adelaide, and
Hobart, as well as at Sydney; and one or two women professors of great distinction have appeared. These, however,
are not the only new portents.

In addition, Australia and New Zealand have taken on the
role of educators for the South-east Asian region and the
South Pacific Islands. Under the Colombo Plan thousands
and thousands of students from these regions are acquiring
Australian 'know-how' at Australian expense – a generous
gesture that is little appreciated in Britain. If these universities are to serve as laboratories for the whole region, they
will need centres of the kind represented by the new International House at Sydney; for students from overseas require something more than a mere hall of residence. The
University of New Guinea and the projected University of
the Pacific at Fiji will become cultural dependencies of Australia and New Zealand for many years. They in turn will
be in search of identity, and if they seek it with the help
of their friends, a new Graduate Society of the Pacific
may in time emerge. But it will emerge only in the
fully shared life, not simply on the exchange of 'know-
how'.

In the educational development of the youngest continent,
I found an enlarged version of that educational progress long
familiar to me from the story of women's education in
Britain. The faithful copying of an admired model can be
seen in the Great Hall of Sydney – and in the Tower at
Girton, which so sedulously reproduces a gatehouse (except
that its base is Tudor, its summit Norman). The heroic attempt to produce as many students as possible, under conditions of austerity, and with some neglect of more advanced

studies was equally familiar. Full maturity produces a break-
away; some repudiation of older traditions; but always, and
continuing, the difficult search for a new identity.

IV

It might be felt that the older universities of England in
general are equally seeking a new identity. Relations between colleges and universities in the modern world are subject to many permutations and combinations; the identity
of a college as of a university is not fixed, but varies with the
larger educational structure and the pressures of society.

As for the student, a woman Principal of long experience
has said:

> The student seeks an instant meaning . . . perhaps he is right in
> believing only through the confrontation of human beings at
> their most personal can he discover a pattern for himself which
> might help to inform the whole of life.*

What are the characteristics of the new educational pattern
in Britain?

That policy which has produced the comprehensive
schools is bound to affect the universities (schools feel that
they must adapt themselves to the expectations of the university whilst universities feel also that they have to adapt themselves to what the schools offer. This process leads to endless
discussion.)

If the education of an *élite* is to be replaced by a more
general education, some risks already discerned in Australia

* Rosemary Park – see footnote on p. 127; the next quotation is also
from the same speech.

and America cannot be discounted and must be anticipated. It is these democratic societies that now begin to insist:

> that it is a privilege to be a student and not a right, that the university is no welfare state open to all, but only to those who will develop intellectual conscience and accept the discipline that comes from specialised knowledge.

The efforts of adaptation made by our older universities have mostly been in the direction of increasing specialisation. New colleges recently founded include one for social science at Oxford and one predominantly for natural science at Cambridge (Nuffield and Churchill): a number devoted to graduates students only; one for women and one for overseas students (New Hall and St Anthony's). Against specialisation, particularly against the idea of postgraduate study being centralised, there is heard the Demon Envy, disguised as Equality of Opportunity, proclaiming that certain universities will take undue prominence, drain too much talent. (However, it is likely that the recent Government economies in postgraduate grants will tend to centralisation, as less costly.)

More collegiate societies have been founded in the last dozen years at Cambridge, than at any time since the Renaissance – some by general effort, some by other colleges, some by individual benefaction. At Oxford and Cambridge, colleges draw together for undergraduate teaching, and form 'cluster' systems. It is necessary to reach an agreed policy on fees, which means an agreed policy on the amount of college teaching. The chief justification of the college is its decentralisation both of studies and of administration to a point where there is virtually no need for a separate administrative class; however costly of time and energy, personal relations are the basis of the system. If colleges are to meet the new challenge

– that of absorbing the alienation, the protest of the younger generation – deeper kinds of agreement must be sought. Attitudes of protest, however generally expressed, are personal; they can be responded to only by those in sympathy with the whole range of student interests.

'Mutual friendship and amity' alone can lead to 'the extirpation of rancour and quarrels' – the aim of that ancient group at Bologna, reinterpreted in terms of our time. New collegiate societies very readily take over the trappings of older colleges, which some of the young have found irksome – the High Table, the silver plate, cap and gown, honorary degrees. (Two critics of the Oxford and Cambridge colleges have admitted that they provide 'an oasis in a colourless world'.) But they form along lines of power, not across them.

An oasis, however brightly coloured, is not what the new society of the protesters require. In the world of the 'cop outs', new symbols of unity have evolved. If in older societies the shared meal once symbolised a way of life, a cafeteria does not necessarily provide a complete alternative; nor does a 'Be-In'. The modern sharers, 'having no judge but themselves', must accept responsibilities, among which are the discovery of new and relevant social forms.

At Oxford and Cambridge, experiments in forms proliferate; Girton has established a link with the second oldest of the men's colleges, Clare, and its offspring, the mixed graduate society of Clare Hall. It is still too early to say what will emerge; at present the sharing of meals, and some common room facilities, for junior members are proposed for 1969.

It may be that the ancient formula of 'the Master, Fellows and Scholars' should be given more reality; that students' demands for an increasing share in government could most readily be met by admitting them to a larger share in small societies than to a smaller share in large societies. This, of course would not please student politicians, but it might assuage deeper disquiet.

'Do you want representation or power?', one of the Berkeley strikers was asked, to which he replied: 'Oh, don't let's get hung up about *words*.'

Colleges, in the modern educational world, should aim at being centres of representation rather than centres of power; they exist for 'unity, company and fellowship' a unity large enough to accept conflict. Protest meetings should be set at the hearth. Formal admission to a college is or should be a true commitment, so that all admitted should be given duties which will make them feel that this is so. This is 'the confrontation of human beings at their utmost personal', but it is not a life of privilege.

In such duties and in such society, lies the antidote to that most deadly form of protest – withdrawal. The bland, infantile 'beautiful person' with a bead necklace and a private Nirvana is not unknown in England. Disaffiliates of this kind, who have turned away from the discipline of knowledge and the labour of creating, have been reclaimed elsewhere in small groups where speech is frank, and where, on occasion, communal judgement is not withheld.*

Education frequently is born in violence; violence is generated either by attempts to withhold or to gain it, for the appetite for knowledge is as powerful as the appetite for

---

* For an account of the situation see J. I. Simmons and Barry Winograd, *Its Happening* (Sta Barbara, 1966.) The extreme of authoritarianism is found in the society for the reclamation of drug addicts, known as Synanon, which claims a 40 per cent rate of cure.

food. Since Eve ate the apple, knowledge has exercised compulsion on man and woman.

Today, education is a political issue, touched with the added irrational fierceness of political hopes and fears.* In many parts of the world, if not in most, educational indoctrination is seen as a major instrument of government. Corruption of the best produces the worst.

Therefore, only while the inevitability of conflict, struggle, distress is accepted as the price of growth and liberal development, will the tradition of Girton's founders be preserved, the sense of wonder and joy that new life brought them remain undiminished.

* The widespread student revolts of 1968 shewed that students could quickly codify their procedure, for in very different circumstances a common pattern of behaviour appeared.

SOME LEADING EVENTS

I. Women's Education in the Nineteenth Century

1843   Governesses' Benevolent Institution founded.

1847   C. Brontë, *Jane Eyre*; Tennyson, *The Princess*; Thackeray, *Vanity Fair*.

1848   F. D. Maurice founds Queen's College, Harley Street.

1849   Mrs Reid founds Bedford College.

1850   Miss F. M. Buss at North London Collegiate School. C. Brontë, *Villette*.

1855   The Ladies' College, Cheltenham founded. Mme. Bodichon's school founded.

1857   Social Science Association founded. First agitation about Women's Franchise.

1859   Elizabeth Garrett meets Emily Davies. Society for Promoting the Employment of Women. Victoria Press founded.

1860   Elizabeth Garrett enters the Middlesex Hospital. Emily Davies, *Letter to a Newspaper*.

1862   London University rejects admission of women to degrees by one vote. Emily Davies moves to London, joins Langham Place circle.

1863   Cambridge Local Examinations opened to women. The Misses Metcalfe's school at Highgate opened.

1864   Cambridge Local Examinations conceded permanent right to examination. Government enquiry on schools begins.

1866   Elizabeth Garrett qualifies as a physician.

Emily Davies applies for secretaryship of Queen's College.

1866 Commission on schools concluded.

London sets special examination for women over 18 years of age.

Petition on suffrage organized and presented to Parliament by J. S. Mill.

1867 North of England Council for Higher Education of Women established.

The College for Women proposed.

1868 Special Examination for Women established by Cambridge Higher Local Examinations.

Emily Davies presents plans for the College for Women to the Social Science Association.

1869 The College for Women opens at Hitchin.

J. S. Mill, *The Subjection of Women.*

1870 The Education Act.

First Hitchin Students pass the Little-Go.

Emily Davies and Elizabeth Garrett Anderson elected to the London School Board.

1871 Henry Sidgwick opens a residence for women in Cambridge.

Plans to move the College for Women to Girton.

1872 Girls' Public Day School Trust founded.

Girton College registered as company with the Board of Trade.

1873 First women students pass Tripos Examinations (March).

Girton College opened (October).

Oxford Committee for Women's Lectures set up.

1875 Newnham Hall opens.

1877 St Leonards School, St Andrews opened.

Maria Gray Training College opened.

1878 London University examinations opened to women.

1878 Oxford association for women students founded.

1879 Lady Margaret Hall, Oxford, and Somerville College, Oxford, opened.

1880 Victoria University, Manchester, founded and opened to women.

1881 Liverpool University opened.
Cambridge passes Graces admitting women to examinations for Tripos, 24 February.

1882 Westfield College, London, founded.
Queen's College, Harley Street, ceases to present for degrees.

1884 Oxford examinations opened to women.

1886 St Hugh's College, Oxford, founded.

1887 Royal Holloway College founded.

1893 St Hilda's Hall, Oxford, founded.

1896 Wycombe Abbey School founded.

1897 Cambridge University rejects Graces for admitting women to degrees.

2. *Women at Cambridge; and Girton College after 1900*
(i) *Constitution*

1904 Emily Davies retires as Secretary of the College Executive Committee.
Education Board created in the college.
Constance Jones, Mistress and member of Executive Committee.

1906 Eleanor Margaret Allen, resident Bursar.

1908 Mary Clover, Secretary, removes to Cambridge from London.

1909 Archdeacon Cunningham, first permanent Chairman of Executive Committee.

SOME LEADING EVENTS

1910   M. T. Meyer appointed Staff representative to Committee.

1910   Pension scheme for staff established.
First Girton Fellowship founded.

1911   Former students establish Roll Association of College Members. Old Girtonians' Studentship founded.
Executive Committee becomes College Council.

1913   Hugh Anderson, Chairman of Council.

1916   K. Jex Blake, Mistress.
Women admitted to M.B. examinations.

1919   Arthur Berry, Chairman of Council.
Jubilee celebrations.
Ethel Sargant Studentship founded for Science.
Yarrow Fellowships established for Science.
Cassell Fund established.
Women admitted to full membership at Oxford.
Royal Commission on Universities, with women's colleges included.

1920   Cambridge University rejects proposal to admit women (December).

1921   Grace admitting women to titular degrees passed.
Carlisle scholarships founded.
Peter Giles, Chairman of Council.

1922   Bertha Phillpotts, Mistress; Royal Commission reports, Statutory Commission set up to implement it; Bertha Phillpotts sole woman member.

1924   First Royal Charter granted to Girton College.

1926   University offices and prizes open to women.

1930   Cambridge Women's Appointments Board founded by Girton and Newnham Colleges.

1948   Women admitted to full membership of the University.

1952 Supplemental Charter and New Statutes granted to Girton College.

1954 New Hall founded.

(ii) *Building*

1873 First block of Girton College (East half of Old Wing).

1876 Old Wing, half of Hospital Wing, Taylor's Knob, College Laboratory.

1880 Gate Lodge.

1884 Completion of Hospital Wing, Orchard Wing, Stanley Library, Old Kitchens (total number now 80 students).

1887 Tower Wing.

1897– Chapel and Woodlands Wings, Hall and Chapel
1902 (total numbers now 180).

1902 Crewdson field bought.

1922 Grange annexe hired (purchased 1926).

1930–
1932 New Wing, McMorran Library and Fellows' Rooms.

1962 Mistress's flat.

1967 Library Annexe.

LIST OF BOOKS

(i) *General*

The best general book is Ray Strachey, *The Cause*, Bell & Sons, London, 1928.

A very full bibliography by O. R. McGregor, in *The British Journal of Sociology*, VI, 1955, pp. 48 ff., is entitled *The Social Position of Women in England, 1850–1914*.

(ii) *Girton College*

Anon, *Emily Townshend*, privately printed, 1936.

Anon, *Gwendolen Crewdson*, privately printed, 1914.

Burton, Hester, *Barbara Bodichon, 1827–1891*, John Murray, London, 1949.

Butler, K. T., and McMorran, H. I., eds., *Girton College Register 1869–1946*, privately printed, 1948.

Dunlop, O. J., *Leaves from a Cambridge Notebook*, Heffer, Cambridge, 1907.

Firth, C. B., *C. L. Maynard*, Allen & Unwin, London, 1949.

Lloyd, Edyth M., *Anne Lloyd*, The Layton Press, London, 1928.

Lumsden, Louisa, *Yellow Leaves*, Blackwood & Sons, London, 1933.

Manton, Jo (Mrs Gittings), *Elizabeth Garrett Anderson*, A. & C. Black, London, 1965.

Mitford, Nancy, ed., *The Ladies of Alderley*, Chapman & Hall, London, 1938. Reprinted 1967.

Roberts, C. H., *The Radical Countess: the Letters of Rosalind, Countess of Carlisle*, Steel Bros., Carlisle, 1962.

Sharp, Evelyn, *Hertha Ayrton*, Constable & Co, London, 1926.

LIST OF BOOKS

Stephen, Barbara, *Emily Davies and Girton College,* Constable & Co., London, 1927.

Stephen, Barbara, *Girton College, 1869–1932,* Cambridge University Press, 1933.

(iii) *The University*

Winstanley, D. A., *Unreformed Cambridge* (1935), *Early Victorian Cambridge* (1940), *Later Victorian Cambridge* (1947), Cambridge University Press.

(iv) *The Lighter Side*

Bobbitt, M. R., *With Dearest Love to All: Life and Letters of Lady Jebb,* Faber & Faber, London, 1960.

Brown, V. E. L., *The Silver Cord,* privately printed, 1952.

Girton Review, The, 1882–

List, E. B., *Girton, My Friend,* Simpkin, Marshall, London, 1908.

Megson, B., and Lindsay, Jean, *Girton College an Informal History,* Heffer, Cambridge, 1960.

Mumford, E. Reid, *Through Rose Coloured Spectacles,* Backus, Leicester, 1952.

Raverat, Gwen, *Period Piece,* Faber & Faber, London, 1952.

Emily Davies's occasional works were edited by
E. E. C. Jones in 1910 as *Questions relating to Women,*
Bowes and Bowes, Cambridge.

INDEX

(i) Persons (publications are entered under authors' names)

INDEX

INDEX

(ii) Institutions

INDEX